Unconventional Wisdom

Conversations About Courage, Growth, and Change

Pat Quigley

CORDILLERA PRESS, INC.
Publishers in the Rockies

Library of Congress Cataloging-in-Publication Data

Quigley, Pat.
Unconventional wisdom.

Bibliography: p.
1. Life. 2. Conduct of life. I. Title.
BD431.Q58 1988 158'.1 88-3538
ISBN 0-917895-21-5

Printed in the United States of America

ISBN: 0-917895-21-5

First Edition
1 2 3 4 5 6 7 8 9

Cover design by Richard M. Kohen, Shadow Canyon Graphics
Typography by Shadow Canyon Graphics, Evergreen, Colorado

Cover painting, "*Crestone Needle – 14,197 Feet*" by R.L. Wogrin, part of the "Highest of the High" series. From the private collection of Mr. Harold Lee.

Cordillera Press, Inc., P.O. Box 3699, Evergreen, Colorado 80439
(303) 670-3010

Table of Contents

Acknowledgements

I wish to thank:

Dr. Charles Crown, long-time friend and purveyor of excellent ideas, who suggested the concept for this book.

Teresa Jordan, friend and author who encouraged me, and whose book, *Cowgirls: Women of the American West* (Anchor Press, 1982), gave me courage to try this interview-oral history format.

Judy Bucher, skillful editor, good friend, who banished ambiguity and trimmed verbosity.

Susan Lewis, extraordinary typist and enthusiastic commentator.

Carolynn Conley, my "left-brained" friend, and Naomi Penner, a fellow soul and writer. Both read chapters and made wise comments on the developing manuscript.

My husband Jack, who underwrites my dreams with almost no complaints.

My son Matt, who offered insightful comments and did extra chores.

My son Tim, who understood my attachment to the typewriter and offered encouraging hugs.

My mother and father, Mary and Jerome Anderson, who extended unqualified belief as only parents know how.

My husband's parents, Margaret and Sam Quigley, who have always made me feel a part of their family.

Dr. Alan Levine, who swept the cobwebs away with thoroughness and gentleness.

Connie Ning, my crony, who exchanged ideas and encouragement.

Nancy Siebold, who has colored my life cheerful with her caring.

Other friends, all dear — all different in their unique support. Carol Benson, Jean and Jim Bilodeau, Nora Dorn, Barbara Eckrote, Mary Gunn, Mary Lou Hodel, Linda Hogan, Parmod Malik, Dorothy Manley, Anne Munson, Ann Platt, Ruth Rice, Verna Rinne, Alice Wescott Robertson, Gary Siebold, Cecile Zupon.

Rocky Mountain Women's Institute, whose early support solidified my commitment to the craft of writing.

Finally, the wise and insightful men and women interviewed, whose stories are not included because of page limitations. I carry their wisdom with me and appreciate their sharing.

Portions of the interviews with Joanne Greenberg, Don Laws, Reynelda Muse, and Pat Schroeder appeared in a different form in *Colorado Homes & Lifestyles* magazine. I appreciate the cooperation of publisher Garrett Giann in using these excerpts here.

To Jack, who is both caring and wise,
in celebration of the newness of
our old love

Foreword

There is a "Peanuts" cartoon strip in which Charlie Brown is standing on the pitcher's mound, surrounded by his players, all of whom are telling him what to do at a critical point in a baseball game. "The world is filled with people who are anxious to act in an advisory capacity," he observes.

The subjects of Pat Quigley's interviews are just the opposite — people who exhibit a certain unconsciousness of role, influencing others with no deliberate attempt to do so. As a research psychologist, I have been intrigued by the personality traits that lead us unerringly to identify wisdom in our leaders, our colleagues, our friends. Such people have an understandable and simple standard of personal conduct that invariably attracts the attention and admiration of other people.

We find this true of the subjects of these interviews. On the pages of this book you will find courage, willpower, flexibility of mind, and integrity. You will not find perfection, but you will meet people who will bring you laughter, tears, and reflections of your own life. They each will leave you with a bit of their personal philosophy and psychology — windows to wise souls.

Neil A. Johnson, Ph.D

All truly wise thoughts have been thought already thousands of times; but to make them truly ours, we must think them over again honestly, till they take root in our personal experience.

Goethe

Preface: No Man or Woman Is Wise Enough Alone

Putting a meaning into life is always a "do-it-yourself" job.
— Joanne Greenberg, novelist

The trick in life is to get through life like a swan. Above the water you look as if you're calm, but underneath, you're paddling like mad.
— Pat Schroeder, U. S. Congresswoman

The only people who are successful in everything they do are the ones who never do anything.
— Ed Kurz, lawyer and small claims court referee

Focus on what you've got, rather than on what you've lost.
— Dale Coski, ex-policewoman and consultant for Denver Commission on the Disabled

I don't need other people's approval so much as I need just to do my best. I don't need to worry about comparing myself with anybody else.
— Randy Gradishar, ex-Denver Bronco linebacker and president of Denver Broncos Youth Foundation

If we want to have joy we have to find it where we are, right *now*.
— Chet Hover, housewife, mother, and grandmother

Do your conversations typically center around work-related issues, the weather, the economy, what's for dinner, or other equally functional, everyday topics? More often than I would like, mine do. It took a project like this book to give me time and opportunity — to hand me an excuse — to sit down and listen, really listen, to others share deeply both their life experiences and philosophies of living.

In these pages you will find interviews with people of unconventional wisdom — that is, individuals who possess out-of-the-ordinary insight, good sense, and judgment. I wrote this book because I believe that wisdom, like despair or depression, is contagious. A negative mindset can be picked up almost anywhere. I wanted to catch, instead, some optimism, some hope, some fresh insights from people who are living their lives wisely and well.

How did I find these people? When setting out to seek individuals with "out-of-the-ordinary insight, good sense, and judgment," the yellow pages don't help. As I pondered how I would recognize the people I wanted to interview, I read and re-read the Old Testament Book of Proverbs, dwelling on King Solomon's wise sayings. I examined Jesus' teachings in the New Testament, then turned to other books — from the ancient *I Ching* to modern volumes by authors such as Sheldon Kopp, Paul Tillich, Madeleine L'Engle, M. Scott Peck, and Anne Morrow Lindbergh. (A partial listing of these is included at the end of this book.)

These sources validated my personal belief that wise men and women are those who, independent of current cultural trends, are committed to *loving both their neighbors and themselves*. They are the balancers — those who nurture themselves and other people too.

There was one other practical consideration, an absolute essential that the prospective interviewees needed to possess. Everyone with whom I talked had to be both willing and able to articulate their personal insights and ideas. "Anyone trained in language can tell you facts, but damn few people can tell the truth or have the courage to be one's self," said contemporary poet Maya Angelou (*USA Today*, "Inquiry," Maya Angelou interviewed by Johnson Lancaster, March 5, 1985).

Angelou was talking about writers. In a sense, those with whom I talked "wrote" their own stories by allowing me to tape their thoughts and publish them here. That took considerable courage. The courage to be themselves — not to try and appear flawless, not to hide behind cliches and generalities, but to specifically and honestly disclose parts of themselves.

My original idea was to include men and women from all over the country. But early along, I found so many people close by that I never left my home state. Some are people I know. I met others while interviewing them for articles in *Colorado Homes and Lifestyles* magazine. I read about a few in the newspaper. Finally, once friends and acquaintances heard about the book, people kept pulling me aside, saying, "I know someone you really should include . . ." As a long-time Colorado resident, I feel a certain pride in this Colorado connection. Yet, though their stories are colored with the Colorado locale, their wisdom is more universal than regional.

But while these people have much in common, the range of ideas and insights in these pages varies as much as the flowers that bloom in a high country meadow. You will not find just one variety of wisdom planted here — not just Roman Catholic thought or "born again" Christian thought or Judaic thought; not just humanistic philosophy or feminist philosophy or pacifist philosophy or any particular prepackaged ideological thought; not just one single political stance or one racial heritage; and certainly not just one age group. Dale Coski, the youngest person, is in her twenties; the oldest, Helen Marie Black, is an octogenarian.

Finally, another difference worth noting. *Unconventional Wisdom* is not a showcase for "celebrity wisdom," nor is it a gathering of "everyday, ordinary people" only. Some of the people here are famous. Others are not. Wisdom does not seem to have much to do with status or reputation.

While writing this book, my own life took many turns. At times, I was managing things well enough, thank you. And it was during these periods that I felt so smug as to wonder why I ever thought of asking anyone else for their insights . . . who needed *them*? But more often, I arrived at an interview in need of a transfusion of hope, courage, or some insight that might help me through a difficulty, decision, hurt, or dilemma.

"Sometimes just being alive feels like raw flesh . . . vulnerable, responsive, irritable, in constant danger," writes Sheldon Kopp. "Those are the times when I most need to sense my place among other people, to hear their tales and know that they are mine as well," he concludes.

I hope that you sense your place in these exceptionally human tales, and that you will see, in some ways you have not seen before, how to live your life more wisely and well.

Helen Marie Black: I Thought I Could

Through the arts the voice
of God speaks to us.
— Source Unknown

Helen Marie Black has forgotten who originated her favorite quote, but she puts a lot of stock in it. For over fifty years, Denver's "grande dame of the arts" has poured energy into diverse artistic enterprises, from helping to launch the Central City Opera to cofounding the Denver Symphony Orchestra to organizing the Red Rocks music festivals. When you consider that she did all this, not as a moneyed matron, but as a single working woman of ordinary means, her accomplishments seem especially amazing.

When I arrive at Black's apartment in Denver's old Capitol Hill neighborhood late one fall afternoon, I find her already dressed for an evening out. She wears a simple, long-sleeved, navy-blue dress with a single strand of pearls. A delicate sculptured hat with a short net holds her white hair in place. A handsome woman in her eighties (she will not divulge her exact age), she is as elegant as the gracious living room where we sit.

It has taken several months of determined effort on my part to get Black to find an empty niche in her schedule for this interview. She is active in the Denver Lyric Opera Guild and the Denver Woman's Press Club, and she goes out regularly with friends, as she is this evening.

I have come with lots of questions. What was it like to be a female reporter in the predominately male city room at the *Rocky Mountain News* in the 1920s? Later, how did she hold down an advertising job while organizing and developing a symphony orchestra in her "spare" time? What kind of philosophy underlies this focused energy?

Before we begin, I ask her when we need to wind up the interview. "We have *plenty* of time," she answers, "several hours." Staring intently at me with her huge eyes, setting me at ease in her quiet and dignified way, she continues. "When we finish, I'm going out to dinner, but I'm all ready." She pauses. "After dinner, we're off to the Symphony. The Symphony's my baby, you know," she says affectionately.

Those involved with the Symphony return Black's affection. In 1983, in conjunction with the fiftieth anniversary of the founding of the Symphony, Black was declared a "public treasure" at a black-tie dinner held in her honor. Out of that tribute came an ongoing award, the Helen Black Arts & Letters Award, to be given annually to other individuals who have made outstanding contributions to the arts in Colorado.

Though a doer, friends point out that Black has never lost sight of people. "She always had time to listen," Dolores Plested, a long-time friend and retired Denver journalist, says.

"Musicians with the Symphony would go to her with their problems — drinking, divorces, whatever. More than once, she bailed some out of jail."

Friends and acquaintances still show up seeking her counsel. "If they come, I don't see how I can turn them away, do you?" she asks me, sounding so sincere and convincing that I automatically nod in agreement.

Our discussion begins. Several times the phone rings and it becomes apparent that while she has an abundance of sympathy to give, when there is a task to accomplish — or an interview to complete — she is single-minded and not easily distracted. "Let it ring," she says, matter of factly, without ever appearing to lose her train of thought even momentarily.

Conversations

Tell me about the early part of your life.

I was born in Washington, D.C. When we moved to Denver I was about to enter high school. My father was a mining engineer and we had lived in New York, Chicago, and Salt Lake City. My mother held a degree in medicine from Johns Hopkins University and was one of the first women in this country qualified to practice medicine. She was a remarkable woman. She had lived in Europe and had been educated like a boy. She knew enough Greek to translate the New Testament from that language into English.

One of her relatives was the poet Sidney Lanier, and I grew up with a love for all of the beautiful things. She opened up the world of art, books, and music to me. My mother never practiced medicine, but devoted all her energy to her family. (Black had one brother, Judge William Alden Black, member of the state legislature in Colorado, and one sister, Blanche Ceselia, "an artistic woman" who married Warren Burgess.)

Why, with this background, didn't you go to college instead of work?

My family was having some financial difficulties when I graduated from Manual High School. I was only sixteen, but I wanted to be a reporter. I figured I would have to have more training, so I went to the *Rocky Mountain News* to find out what I would need to do to become one. Instead of giving me information, they ended up giving me a job.

My mother was shocked. She thought that my going to work was terrible, but we did need the money. I was paid five dollars a week. We had no union rules and we'd sometimes work forty-eight hours at a stretch. I was the first and only female reporter on the news staff, other than the society editor.

I didn't dress in men's clothes. I stayed feminine, and I found the men never took advantage of me. They were most helpful.

I loved every minute of that job. When I was still in my teens I covered the 1924 Democratic Convention at Madison Square Garden. There were many "great ones" there. I sat in back of Will Rogers. A lawyer, John W. Davis, won the nomination on the 103rd ballot. Of course, Calvin Coolidge was reelected.

Did the fact that you were so young cause any problems?

Only once. The head of the women's suffrage movement came to town when I was starting out. There was to be a big meeting and the city editor sent me to cover the story. When I arrived she said, "*Well,* you're too young to interview me." I said, "*Well*, my editor sent me. *He* thinks I can do it." "You're *too* young," she shot back. So, I told my editor and he said, "Go tell her that either you do it, or the paper won't cover her at all." I did. I got the interview.

When I was sixteen people would say, you're too young to do this, you're too young to do that — too young and too pretty. Since age was such a deterrent, I decided right then never to have one! And I haven't. I've never since felt too young or too old to do anything.

Who are some of the "greats" you interviewed?

I talked with Lindbergh. After he flew the Atlantic (May 21, 1927), he came back to the States and made a tour of the cities, including Denver. He stayed at the Brown Palace, and all the papers and wire services gathered for one big press conference.

Well, I wanted more than that kind of impersonal interview, so I asked him afterwards, "Would you give me five minutes all by yourself?" He said yes.

We went to his suite and sat down on the floor with a map. He traced the route of his flight for me. I said to him, "You're more comfortable in the air than on the earth, aren't you? You're a 'bird man,' I think."

He answered, "Yes, I am." So that's how I began my story.

When Helen Keller was here, my editor wanted me to stay with her for the entire week and bring back a story every day. I did. One evening I took her to a performance of Gallagher and Shean. They were a comedy team who performed in the Ziegfield Follies. They were in a musical at the Broadway Theater in Denver. I called the manager there and asked, "Would you please save the first box seat for Helen Keller?" He said, "She can't hear what goes on." I said, "You wait. Put her in the front box." He did. It was amazing. She laughed in the right places. Poor Gallagher and Shean were in a tizzy.

I also interviewed the evangelist Amy Semple McPherson in 1921. She was preaching at a temple on Curtis Street. Ray Colvin, the *News* city editor, sent me to cover her — the men on the paper had been there and had come back with nothing. When I went, I couldn't believe what I saw. People were actually turning cartwheels down the aisles just to get to her to be healed.

That was the lead for my story, which turned out to have an eight-column headline on page one. So Colvin told me to stay with her, too, and bring back a story each day. I took her up to Lookout Mountain and asked her to do a Sermon on the Mount. That attracted a lot of attention. I also took her to visit some shut-ins. One happened to be a relative of Harry Tammen — he founded the *Denver Post*. We took McPherson in to pray over this sick person, who happened to be staying at Tammen's house, and while she did, Tammen bowed his head in prayer, too. This was rather startling because Tammen was a villain — he was *not* known for being "nice."

My headline the next day read "HARRY TAMMEN BOWS HIS HEAD IN PRAYER." When Tammen saw that he called me. "What the hell did you mean by saying I bowed my head in prayer?" he screamed. I said, "Well, that's the nicest thing that's ever been said about you. I'd think you'd thank me." We kept on talking and he ended up offering me a job at the *Post*! I covered the rest of Aimee's story in Mr. Tammen's limousine. He provided a box lunch and five pounds of candy from Bauers Candy Store every day.

(Black still sounds delighted at pulling off such a coup. Besides this victory, she is also credited with taking McPherson from relative obscurity into national fame with her series of stories that week.)

After your years as a reporter, you went into advertising?

Yes. I worked as advertising consultant at the Denver Dry Goods. Then I was assistant advertising manager at Daniels and Fisher, which later was bought by the May Company. Finally, I had my own agency. I did publicity for just about everything imaginable. During World War II, I received a citation from the government for doing such a good job publicizing the Red Cross blood drive.

And while you were working in advertising, you founded the Symphony?

Yes. In 1933, Denver had a Civic Symphony made up of both amateur and professional musicians. What we set out to do was to organize a symphony of *all* professionals. (Lucille Wilkin and Mrs. George Cramner also participated in that organization.) Even though the Depression was on in a big way, and even though musicians were literally starving, we managed to do this and to pay them union wages.

Tell me about your work with the Symphony after the initial organization.

I served as its business manager and promoter. For the first twelve years I worked as a volunteer. After that I was paid a salary.

I had no "job description;" I just did whatever needed doing. I helped the musicians negotiate new contracts. I booked tours for the Symphony, and when visiting artists came into town to appear with the Symphony, I met them at the airport or train station. I made arrangements for their hotels, made sure there were flowers in their rooms, escorted them to parties in their honor, and arranged radio or television interviews for them.

And then there was always the fund raising. I would go to individuals and just talk with them and tell them how important it was that we bring culture to Denver. And even if they did not especially appreciate classical music or a symphony, they would understand and almost always make a contribution.

I always had ideas for publicity. We started the Red Rocks Music Festival series in the mid-forties. And it was just amazing! When a singer came to that beautiful outdoor setting, the birds would often come out during the performance and sit on top of the huge rock that towered above the stage.

When Lily Pons appeared at Red Rocks, I came up with an idea that I hoped would gain national publicity. Well, I thought, Lily has a voice like a bird and if the birds will fly out when she sings, what a marvelous picture. I called the *Life* magazine bureau in Denver. They thought it was a great idea. They said they'd have a photographer there.

But then I began to worry — what if the birds don't show up? Well, my friend Dolores and I called all over until we found some pigeons. We put them in a crate and took them to the concert.

Pons sang, but no birds appeared, so just as she struck a high "C" we released the pigeons. They got a picture of Pons with the birds. We made *Life* with that one!

When I left the orchestra in 1963, it had become nationally known. Saul Caston, a former conductor of the Philadelphia Philharmonic, had become conductor in 1945 and was here until 1963. By the time I left, the Symphony had even been featured in a movie shown at the World's Fair in Belgium. I went to Belgium to see it. I really felt quite satisfied then that the Symphony was known the world over.

And all this time you worked fulltime, too? How did you do it?

I look back and I don't know. There was a lot of work to do to keep the orchestra going. Sometimes I would be up all night working. I didn't sleep or eat much. I had migraine headaches. I didn't do anything else like playing bridge. But I was having such a good time, I just never thought about it. I just did it.

Why has there been so little publicity about you until recently?

If you're promoting yourself, I don't see how you can really do a good job of promoting whatever you're promoting. All those years working with the Symphony, I never once gave my name to a newspaper. I had the conductor announced, the president of the board announced, and a committee person announced, but never myself. I just wanted the work to get done. I wanted the orchestra to be in the spotlight.

What's your pet project now?

I'm involved with the Denver Lyric Opera Guild. I liked to help young artists during my era with the orchestra. (Among those whose careers she helped to boost are pianist Van Cliburn and violinist Eugene Fodor.) Now I'm working on their education committee. The Guild provides travel expenses and money so that the singer can go and audition in New York at the Metropolitan Opera. The Guild also pays for singing lessons.

Your spirit is exceptionally unselfish.

My actions all stem from my belief that if I try to be unselfish and grateful, then God will go before me and prepare a way — that I will be taken care of. And I have been.

When I was just sixteen, my city editor said to me, "Go out and get three Sunday feature stories." At first I thought, where will I go? Where? Well, I asked God to guide me. He did. I got those three stories, and my editor thought they were great.

I am grateful for everything that comes to me. *Everything.* I know I've been given so much. Every morning I have a prayer period. I always have had. I pray for everybody, not just for myself.

What advice would you give people, based on your experience?

Just get an idea and do it. Put your energy into the cause and put yourself in the background. When people tell you it can't be done, as they will, just think to yourself, I can do it.

I never thought of roadblocks. I had things to do and I just did them. I didn't have time to ask, can I or can't I?

Anybody can accomplish a dream if they feel that way. Don't sit around and waste time asking, "Can I?" Just do it.

Foster & Hermie Cline: Marriage Maintenance

The way Foster and Hermie Cline behave at parties, you'd think they were newlyweds. She holds his hand. He sits close beside her. When one talks, the other listens intently. Theirs is not the half-interested, staring-off-someplace-else habit that married couples seem to acquire as easily as high mortgages and car payments.

Friends, even their children, say this is no act. This couple, about to celebrate their twenty-fifth wedding anniversary, is like this most of the time. They *like* to be together.

But it is not by accident that they still are. Theirs is not a union so well-oiled and perfect that they never fight or struggle. The difference is that they are committed to the daily maintenance necessary for keeping a vintage relationship alive and well.

Foster and Hermie met while they were still students at the University of Colorado in Boulder. They married young. "I was *almost* nineteen and Foster was *almost* twenty," Hermie says.

Foster Cline, a Denver native, is an internationally known psychiatrist who practices in Evergreen, a commuter community in the mountains thirty-five miles west of Denver. His specialty is child psychiatry, but he also does therapy with couples and adults. He travels worldwide giving lectures and conducting workshops on weighty topics such as psychological management of the difficult child. At the time of our conversation, he had just returned from a month in Melbourne, Australia, working for a government residential treatment center for disturbed children.

Besides being a homemaker, Hermie Cline co-leads workshops with Foster, sessions that focus on communication skills and problem-solving techniques for couples. In addition, she plans the itinerary for a travel-study program that they supervise abroad each summer. While Foster was working in Australia, she was touring Germany and

Switzerland, making arrangements for next summer's session.

The Clines have four children. Robin, twenty-four, is married; Andy, twenty-one, is off at college. Two children are still at home. Jerry, fifteen, is a ninth grader. The newest family member is Melinda, age ten, whom Foster and Hermie adopted eighteen months ago.

Now in their early forties, Foster and Hermie Cline look years younger. Both have straight teeth, chiseled features, rosy cheeks, and expressions that seem remarkably tension-free for two people who are still raising children and pursuing busy careers. Out of their extensive professional backgrounds and from twenty-five years of personal practice, here is what they say about the art of being married.

Conversations

After all these years together, how do you keep your romance alive?

Hermie: I'm just a basic romantic. I need to be close, to touch. This morning when Foster and I were in the basement straightening out some things, I was aware that I touched him almost every time I walked past. I'd give him a pat, just some little thing. I like doing that.

Foster: It's an easy way of saying, "I'm here. I care," and really, it takes a lot less energy than saying, "I love you." You can go on about your business and it's fun.

Hermie: He's got the *best* hands to hold. They're always warm, and they're so soft. Just try holding his hand. It's such a nice hand to hold.

Foster: It's easy to be romantic because we *want* to be together. We don't just *need* to be together. She is not dependent on my presence for being happy. It's the same with me. We don't just *need* to be together. I *want* to be with her because I enjoy her.

I always want Hermie to *want* to be with me because she doesn't *need* to be with me. So that means if she ever reaches the point that she doesn't *want* to be with me, she'll *be* with someone else. And that would be a definite bummer! But, we're not always holding hands. We have our times for separateness. I do my thing. Hermie does hers.

When irritations or problems come up, how do you handle them?

Foster: We both bring little things that are upsetting to each other's attention. One of the things I appreciate about Hermie is that she can bring these things up without getting angry.

Hermie, would you show me how you do this?

(After assuring them I would like to see them work on a problem in front of me if they feel comfortable, they seem to forget I'm there. While the following lively discussion may sound like mere role playing — a technique that the Clines use in couple workshops — it is a real interaction about a real problem.)

Hermie: I don't want to complain. . . .

Foster: What's on your mind?

Hermie: Well, I hate to bring this up but I just get tired of your sloppiness.

Foster: Oh . . .

Hermie: I'm really tired of it.

Foster: In what areas?

Hermie: Your Alka Seltzer packages. You left them on the kitchen table this morning.

Foster: Oh, I thought I'd been good about not doing that.

Hermie: For two days you were real good.

Foster: Is that *all*? Two days?

Hermie: That's all. I know you don't consciously do this, saying, "Hermie the maid will come by and clean all this up." But the other day your empty vitamin pill package was on the floor by the chair in the dining room.

Foster: It was?

Hermie: You know — it was as if you had said, "I'm just going to throw my trash here."

Foster: No! I don't usually throw trash on the floor!

Hermie: (quietly) It was there.

Foster: And that's not an exception?

Hermie: No, it's not an exception.

Foster: I'll try and watch that.

Hermie: I hate to bring this up because it's such a little thing. . . .

Foster: I'm sorry. I don't think it's fair that I'm this messy, but I do it *truly* unconsciously.

Hermie: I know that, honey.

Foster: I mean, I don't do it in a chauvinistic way. You know I do things around the house — the dishes, I help with the laundry.

Hermie: I know, but you just weren't trained to be tidy and neat.

Foster: Look, I know I shouldn't *have* to be reminded and I *will* try harder to be neater, but for two days I want you to bring it up every time I'm messy. I'll see if I can handle that, cause I'm sorry about this.

Hermie: Okay. This sounds like a good agreement. I'll start today.

Foster: Okay.

Do you always resolve things like this so smoothly?

Foster: No, and this isn't resolved yet. We will have to keep our promises about doing what we just agreed on. But this was a good time for Hermie to talk to me. If she had brought this up last night, we might not have talked about it so calmly. For a long time we used to try and fight something out when we were both tired.

Hermie: Sometimes even at bedtime we'd say, "*this* (whatever the problem was) needs resolving *now*." Finally we learned that some things that are upsetting at night are not even worth fighting about the next morning. And if the problem is a big deal, then waiting until the next day when we're both rested always helps. Sometimes, though, it's hard to put something aside and wait. It takes effort and restraint.

Foster: It helps to make a clear agreement in the evening to talk about an issue the next morning, *if* we still wish to. Otherwise, the waiting could be used as an escape mechanism for *never* facing things. Both partners must go ahead and face whatever it is that is bothering them the next morning for this to work.

Hermie and I have another rule that we use about settling things — never deal with a chronic problem while the chronic problem is occurring. This applies to a marriage or to dealing with kids. If I'm a grouch in the morning, which I sometimes am, it would be really *tacky* for Hermie to confront me with that in the morning. She can talk to me about being a morning grouch in the *evening* when I'm in a more receptive mood. A therapist will never talk to a person about a drinking problem when that person is drunk. The only person stupid enough to do that is a spouse! And one sure thing about a chronic problem — you always know it's going to come up again!

Why do many married people no longer enjoy each other after a few years together?

Foster: The major thing that keeps people from enjoying a relationship is dwelling on past resentments and worrying about the future. It's easy to start "obsessing" about either. You may look back at something your partner did and keep saying to yourself, "Why did she do that? Why did she do that?" The way the brain works, once you shift into dwelling on some past injury or hurt — large or small — it becomes easier and easier to stay there. You actually make a pathway, a biochemical pathway, in your neurons.

Hermie: You literally become stuck in a rut.

Foster: Getting out might require therapy. It might just require self-discipline and a lot of determination. But whatever it takes, it is worth the effort if you want to stay together.

It's only when you're focusing on the present that you and your partner have something really new to enjoy with each other. If you're thinking about what the future might be, or what the past has been, you're not really alive to the here and now.

Life is supposed to be fun. A marriage is supposed to be fun. I just don't want my life to slide past without having fun!

(After the interview, Foster asks Hermie to leave before he does. She protests and looks a little peeved, but she leaves. Foster tells me about the surprise party he's planning for their upcoming silver anniversary. He has asked the minister who married them to perform another ceremony at the celebration. He has put together a slide show of their years together. He beams like a little boy who has managed to ditch school without being found out.)

Dale Coski: Focusing on What You Still Have

September 12, 1983. 5:30 a.m. Denver police officer Dale Coski has already been patrolling her beat — the Montbello district — for three and a half hours, and she is low on gas. She is driving on Interstate 70, planning to exit to fill up her squad car, when ahead in the tunnel near Stapleton International Airport she notices a car stalled in the far right-hand lane. There is no shoulder in the tunnel. So Dale turns on the flashing overhead lights and pulls in behind the car to assist the driver.

Right away, she finds out that the problem is simple — just a flat tire. She knows the danger of being stopped in that shadowy tunnel and hurries around to the trunk of her squad car. She is about to get out the tools that she needs to help change the tire when without warning a pickup truck that she hears, but never sees, crashes into her, crushing her between it and her squad car.

Dale Coski is rushed to Denver General Hospital, where she remains for six weeks. In addition to massive head injuries, she also has suffered spinal cord damage that has left her paralyzed from the neck down. Her left leg had to be amputated above the knee.

At age twenty-six, in that one irrevocable moment, the one-year veteran of the Denver Police Department had lost it all — everything that had made her life worth living. She had lost her ability to walk or to work as a policewoman, and much, much more.

It is sixteen months after the accident that Dale and I talk one chilly January afternoon. Outside her small, ranch-style house in southwest Denver, the air is heavy and humid, and the sky is swirled with pewter clouds.

Inside, Dale sits in a motorized wheelchair warming herself near a small space heater in the center of the living room. She wears a violet sweatsuit. Her expression is pleasant, her face unlined.

Curled on the floor beside her is a large, ferocious-looking German shepherd. "She won't hurt you," Dale assures me. Percey (short for perseverance) is a service dog, trained especially to help a disabled person, much like a seeing eye dog assists a blind master. She is literally Dale Coski's arms and legs now.

Before the accident, Dale was one of Colorado's top women bowlers. She also played racquetball, basketball, and football, and ran several miles a day. When she joined the Denver Police Department in January 1982, she had already been a nun, a sergeant in the army, and a security guard.

Scattered around Dale's living room are books — *The Joy of Being Human, Better Times Than These*, and paperback novels. Photographs of her in her nun's habit and in an army uniform are on the mantel over a fireplace. In the kitchen, a "Hill Street Blues" calender is hanging on one wall. A different police officer is pictured each month.

Dale Coski is one very stubborn woman with a tough Christian faith. In this interview about her life before and after the accident, there is not much "sweetness and light." Never once does she say that she knows there was purpose in all this or that "this must be God's will." She is angry. Some mornings she has been so despondent that she has refused to be helped out of bed into her wheelchair.

As we talk, she goes out of her way to minimize her bravery, trying to cover her courage by being matter-of-fact and, on occaasion, gruff. But her actions keep speaking louder than her words, just as they always have in her life. Already, she has a new job on the Denver Commission on the Disabled. And, of course, like her previous positions, it is one in which she can help other people. She has a new roommate and other new friends. She has Percey, who "is like a member of the family."

"I am sorry it took reading about your accident in the newspaper for me to find you," I say to Dale before we begin. "You are the kind of person I was looking for anyway." My words seem as inadequate as any I've ever spoken, but Dale accepts them as they were intended, and we begin.

Conversations

Tell me about your background before you became a police officer.

In 1976 I quit Loretto Heights College to become a postulant in the Sisters of the Blessed Sacrament for Indians and Colored People. Essentially this means that I went in training to become a full-fledged nun. At first I was sent to the mother house in Pennsylvania to learn about community living, spiritual direction, discipline, and prayer. I cleaned the chapel each day, and once a week I played my accordian for the older sisters in the nursing home.

Then I was sent to Chicago's south side on a mission experience. Since I didn't have my degree, I was to be a teacher's aide for a class of first-graders. As it turned out, the teacher got sick and I ended up taking over.

I became a nun because I wanted to serve. At that time, this was the only way I could think of to do this. But then my dad died, and I decided I was needed at home. So I left the convent and returned home to help my mom. When things were under control again, I decided to enlist in the army.

They assigned me to military intelligence. I can't tell you about it, and that's one of the reasons why I left. I didn't like not being able to share any of my experiences.

After my discharge I worked in security at the K Mart Corporation in Denver. I was promoted to security manager at a suburban store. I was supposed to pick up shoplifters, but there just weren't that many at that particular store! So I decided to apply to be a policewoman.

Why did police work suit you so well?

I just like helping people. Even writing a ticket is helping somebody, because that person might not break that law again. I tried to write tickets with either zero or low-point violations, because I didn't want people to have sky-high insurance rates. I never wrote a speeding ticket because I sometimes exceeded the speed limit myself. I thought it was hypocritical to write a ticket for something I did.

Was it a problem to handle the job because you're small?

No. I remember one call, for instance, where a guy was "unwanted" in a house. Another policewoman and I were trying to make him leave. He was over six feet tall, and he wouldn't let go of the kitchen chair. Poor Gail was using her night stick to pry his arms loose, but he just wouldn't move.

I finally said, "Gail, move out of the way. I'll get my mace." Both his hands flew up into the air and he yelled, "No, no, no!" We grabbed him real fast and handcuffed him. Later we were commended by the division chief for using so much restraint!

I was a policewoman for less than two years. Thank heavens that when I was hurt, at least I was helping somebody. In a way, that makes it easier.

Tell me about what happened after the accident.

In those six weeks at Denver General, I only remember two things — trying to kick the windows out to get back to work, and talking to my mother. My mother died four months before my accident, and I believe that I really was talking to her. I kept on seeing her and saying, "Mom, take me with you. I want to go with you." And she just answered, "No Dale, but don't worry. I'll be with you. I'll help you get through this."

There have been lots of times since then that I've cussed her out for helping me, 'cause I think it would be a lot easier if I hadn't made it.

At Craig Rehabilitation Center (where she remained for five months as an inpatient and two more as an outpatient), I just thought, if they say I'm going to spend my life in a wheelchair, I'll just stay in bed. So when they told me I would never walk, I wouldn't even let them get me up. I'd find any excuse to avoid sitting in that wheelchair. You should have seen me. I still had my halo (a device used to set the broken spinal cord in the correct position until the bones have healed together). I was on a trach (tracheotomy). I just didn't want to cooperate.

Sometimes even now I feel the same way. When I first moved into my house a few months ago, one of my aides (Dale has physical aides on duty twenty-four hours a day) couldn't come to work until eleven. The phone rang and I went to answer it, and somehow my blanket got tangled in the wheels of my chair. I couldn't go forward. I couldn't go backward. I couldn't get to the phone. The caller happened to be my ex-roommate who knew I was here alone, so when she got no answer, she drove over. She pounded at the door. There was a garage door opener on my chair, but I couldn't get it to work! Finally, she ripped open the screen in the kitchen and came in through a window. By then, I was a mess. That night I wanted very much to call it quits.

Another time, just after I got the van, an aide was driving me to the store. My aide pulled out into traffic and ran into a car. All I could think of was that someone was standing between the car and van, crushed as I had been. I panicked. I kept on yelling, "Let me out of here!" I felt better when I could see that we had just a fender-bender.

What has kept you going?

My friends. In the hospital I always had someone visiting. The people at the police department have really encouraged me. The aides at Craig really helped.

I have to admit, though, that I think everybody at Craig hated me for awhile. I was really mean. I don't usually cuss, but there . . .

I was at Craig on New Year's Eve, and I rang to have my leg bag (storage bag for urine) emptied. The guy answering the intercom said, "Well, we'll send an aide when one's available."

Because of the holiday, they were short that night. Two hours later nobody had come. I called again. By the time an aide came, the bag had busted and urine was everywhere. If it hadn't broken, I could have hyper-reflexed, which is like having a stroke. I was furious!

So for the rest of the night, every ten minutes, I got the guy on the intercom and cussed him out. He kept saying, "We can't have you talking like that." I said, "tough," or something a little stronger! Then I'd hang up and call him again. Somehow being mean was enjoyable.

But the support that so many people have given me has been incredible. I've gotten tons of letters. Unfortunately, the cards were separated from the envelopes, so I can't find all the addresses. But I'm still trying to track down some of them so I can answer.

Tell me about your new job.

I'm working with the Commission on the Disabled in Denver. I'm an intern right now. It will take six to nine months to learn the entire job. There are five of us who work full-time, and our main purpose is to protect the civil rights of disabled individuals and to implement changes that make life easier for anyone with a handicap.

Mainly what I am working on now is examining the accessibility of buildings. By law, all city buildings have to be accessible to the handicapped, and any structure that has received federal funds does, too. But in the past, waivers were granted far too easily. So I look at requests for waivers. And I try to be fair to the architects, but to be fair to the handicapped, too. Our commission makes recommendations about these kinds of access issues.

I'm also working on trying to get something passed in the state legislature so that disabled people can write out their own parking tickets when they find someone illegally parked in a handicapped parking space. In California that is being done now. Another thing, most handicapped parking spaces are the same size as the others, and they need to be larger. Also, the architects need to know more about how to design parking spaces. At one post office the handicapped parking space has the ramp right in front of it, so when you park there, you can't get up the ramp!

There just are so many issues. I had to go to the doctor the other day, and I went into the bathroom that was supposed to be "wheelchair accessible." But the turn-around space wasn't big enough and I couldn't even get in there. We need to educate people. Before this accident, *I* wouldn't have known about such problems.

I wish I could go back and work at the police department in some area of human relations. I would love to teach people about crime watch in their neighborhoods. I would like to educate people about the handicapped and their problems. If there were ever such a position, I would take it in a minute. I was more satisfied, more fulfilled, working as a police officer than I had ever been. I miss it.

Have the recent changes in your life helped — the new job, your roommate, and your dog, Percey?

Definitely. Shelga Williams, my roommate, lived across the street before she moved in. She had never done anything with the handicapped. I didn't even know her before this accident. But one day she came over with a six-pack of beer. I don't drink beer, but I said I'd have some lemonade. So we just sat around talking, and we got to be friends. Her parents still live just across the street, and they're always willing to help out.

They — and Percey (she looks down at her German shepherd) — are my family now. This past Christmas — what a difference from the first one after my accident! Shelga and I went to her parents' home for a fondue dinner on Christmas Eve. Then we went to midnight mass. Percey even went! Then we came back and opened our gifts, then we went to bed for a little while.

The next morning on Christmas, around 11 o-clock in the morning, we went out for a buffet dinner. Later in the day we were back at Shelga's parents' home. It was really nice.

And Percey — how did you find him?

I just happened to find out about the Canine Companions for Independence Program through Nancy Maico, my physical therapist at Craig. She is the best therapist there is! She knew someone in California who was a participant in the program. Her knowledge of this program was perhaps the greatest gift that Craig could have ever given me. (Canine Companions for Independence also trains "social" dogs to provide companionship for frail or disabled people and "signal" dogs to be ears for the deaf. For information, write Canine Companions for Independence, 1215 Sebastopol Road, P.O. Box 446, Santa Rosa, California 95402.)

The whole purpose of this organization is to select and train dogs who can then help people with disabilities. I had to go through a two-week training program with Percey out in Santa Rosa, California.

Percey knows eighty-five commands. She knows how to turn on a light switch, press an elevator button, pay a bill in a restaurant, and pull a wheelchair up a hill. If I drop something, she can pick it up. Watch! (Dale wheels herself into the bedroom and commands Percey to turn on the light switch. Percey whines, disobeying at first, but then performs the task.)

I don't mind that she defies me sometimes. I like an ornery dog. Some people see me that way, too! I went shopping not long ago with an aide and Percey came along. In the checkout, a man kept staring at us. Finally, he asked my aide, looking right past me, "What's her dog's name?" I let it pass this time, but the next time someone ignores me and acts as if I'm deaf, dumb, and retarded. . . .

I'm starting to do a lot of public speaking. A Brownie troop in North Denver asked me to bring Percey to their meeting, speak to them, and just demonstrate what Percey can do. They sent me a Brownie pin for Percey's backpack (used to carry any necessities that Dale needs when they are out). Percey's now an honorary Brownie!

Do you have any advice for people who find themselves in a situation similar to yours?

(Dale hesitates before answering. She answers quietly.)

Focus on what you've got, rather than what you've lost. I try to look at what I still have. When I get mad, I know who to get mad at. That's important, too. And I do get mad as hell about the whole situation. So I cuss out God. Some aides get all shook about that, but the way I feel, God's the ideal one to cuss out. If I were to cuss out the aide or my roommate, they could sit there and take it, and they'd say, "Oh, it's her condition." That's fine, but they can't really understand. So — the one who understands is the one I'm cussing out.

God understands?

That's right. He knows what I'm going through. Even his son Jesus felt the same kind of distress I do. When he was crucified, he said, "My God, my God, why have you forsaken me?" He felt the same thing.

Some people persist in telling me all this is God's will and that I should thank God because all things work out for good. I just let them talk.

I only have three or four days a month that are really bad emotionally. Last week when Shelga came in to check on me — I have her pull the covers up over my head because the way my circulation is now, I get so cold — I had been crying and the sheet was all wet, and she was all shook up. But, as I told her later, the psychologist said that if I didn't have these times I wouldn't be normal.

And just today I finally was able to help Shelga. She was in a minor car accident this morning. All I could think about until I got to the emergency room was oh my God, now she'll be taken away from me. But she just had some stitches in her leg. Bad enough, but she'll be okay. The rest of the family had to leave when they started in with those stitches. I was the only one who could stay in there! I think just "being there" with a person's awfully important.

And I am thankful for all the people who've done that for me.

Betsy Dayton: Balance and Healing

"There's a woman in Denver named Betsy Dayton who practices an ancient oriental healing art called Jin Shin Jyutsu. She's treated me for years for everything from tennis elbow to tension. She has a lot of wisdom about how we can put more balance into our lives, and how we can gain more energy. She ought to be in your book."

This enthusiastic recommendation from a highly energetic acquaintance in her mid-forties prompted me to call Betsy Dayton. Over the phone, she said "yes" to an interview and also invited me to experience a Jin Shin treatment. I asked her to explain a little about Jin Shin Jyutsu and how she came to practice it.

"Jin Shin Jyutsu is a highly developed form of acupressure which originated around four or five thousand years ago," she explained. "It's actually the healing art that *acupuncture* is based on."

"Acupuncture?" I had seen photographs of people with needles jutting from them, but I knew little.

"*Acupuncture* is an old Chinese method of relieving pain and treating disease by inserting needles into various parts of the body," she continued patiently. "But in *acupressure*, we don't insert needles; we use gentle finger pressure on these points."

Dayton went on to explain that all the acupressure techniques are based on the belief that a vital energy force flows in connected pathways or meridians throughout the body. "These are not anatomical pathways like arteries or veins; they lie deeper than that. If a person is totally healthy — mentally, emotionally, and physically — energy will flow uninterrupted through these pathways, much like electricity is conducted through circuits," she said. "But none of us is totally healthy. We all experience disease, injury, and emotional traumas. And there are environmental stresses too, like pollution and noise. The purpose of a treatment is to rebalance or unblock the energy flows throughout the body, so that the body can begin to heal itself."

Dayton was once in a more conventional career. From 1969 to 1976 she worked for the Colorado State Department of Education in Denver, writing grants and designing learning programs for the schools. She has an undergraduate degree in bilingual teaching and community development from the State University at Old Westbury in New York and a masters degree in education from Antioch University. She took a class in Jin Shin Jyutsu in 1975 and started to practice on herself and friends. She felt more and more drawn to it, so quit writing grants and opened a fulltime practice in 1976.

Now, besides Jin Shin (the pet name that practitioners use instead of the longer one), Dayton also uses other forms of healing such as yoga, breathing therapy, homeopathy, and herb and nutrition regimens, according to clients' needs. Currently she divides her time between her Denver office and another on San Juan Island in the Puget Sound off the Washington state coast.

Dayton also travels around the United States, Canada, and Mexico giving treatments and lectures on Jin Shin, and she teaches classes regularly. "For years this healing art was practiced in the home in China and in Japan," she says. "I would like to see this happen here, so one of my main goals is to teach people how to use Jin Shin. Right now around 400 people in Colorado have been trained. To my knowledge, I was the first person in this state to learn Jin Shin." (You can give yourself a Jin Shin Jyutsu treatment or practice this art on someone else. When doing it on someone else, it means "the art of compassionate being." When treating yourself, it is "the art of knowing and helping myself.")

Several weeks after our phone conversation I arrived for the interview and a treatment at Dayton's home office on the west side of Denver. Inside her beige brick bungalow, I found a pleasant waiting area. Healthy plants. Books of poetry and philosophy. Indian pottery and baskets. Soft pale green carpeting and grey walls.

The room, with its collage of textures and muted colors, was serene. A Siamese cat wandered over to rub against my legs. I sat down on a sofa draped with an Indian rug; across from me was a closed door with a small sign that read, "Quiet Please, Sessions Are in Progress."

Soon Dayton opened the door and came out to introduce herself. Her client, a white-haired woman who looked exceedingly relaxed, followed her. After saying goodbye, Dayton invited me into her treatment room.

"Leave your shoes out here if you like," she said, pointing to an area just outside the door. Once inside, she instructed, "Just lie down here." I lay down on my back on a comfortable padded table, fully clothed, as is the practice in Jin Shin.

Quietly, Dayton began to ask questions. "Have you had any surgery? Any injuries? Are you aware of any emotion that you don't express fully?"

After exploring more issues like this, she took hold of my wrist. "Your pulse is like a computer readout of your whole energy system — a tactile readout," she said. "I can pick up the rhythm of a person's energy system and how it is flowing and where it is blocked from the pulse."

Dayton sensed several blockages and began to work. According to Jin Shin, there are twenty-six body release points. Her treatment consisted of pressing these points in various combinations. She touched a point on the back of my neck, for instance, while at the same time pressing another at the back of my knee.

As she employed many such diverse combinations from head to toe, I felt a variety of sensations, some like mild electrical currents, flowing from point to point. Some spots that she touched actually ached and throbbed dully. After an hour of gentle finger pressure mixed with quiet conversation about my lifestyle, complaints, and concerns, it was time for our interview.

During the treatment and the conversation, I found Dayton to be serene. Though she exudes such gentle traits, she seems neither placid nor weak. Behind eyes which sparkle like pieces of pale green jade, something strong and resolute resides. She exhibits the calm confidence of one who has searched for a purpose in her life and found it.

This softly feminine, single woman (she was divorced some years ago) spends as many as fourteen hours a day giving Jin Shin treatments. She seems as confident in its healing power as any skier is certain of finding snow in the Colorado Rockies each January.

While some physicians and mental health therapists will not commit themselves to say that this ancient healing art works, few will say with certainty that it does not. Psychologists and physicians often refer patients who are not responding to conventional treatment to Dayton.

With or without belief in Jin Shin Jyutsu's healing power, Dayton makes a lot of sense as she talks about the balancing of lives.

Conversations

Why did you switch from a career in education to practicing Jin Shin Jyutsu?

My background — the way I grew up — influenced my decision. I grew up in Tucson, Arizona. My parents raised us (her sister, Kate, and brothers, Paul and Eli) with a combination of Quaker thought, Far Eastern philosophy, and a North American Indian respect for the earth, all of nature, and an awe of the universe. Even before I went to school I had done yoga classes and learned meditation from my mother.

My mother (Mona Dayton) is a very unusual person! She was into health foods — brewers yeast, natural whole wheat bread, homemade yogurt — long before these foods were "in."

My mother taught us that the earth is a garden and that there are earth spirits to keep it growing. She told us that clouds would speak to us if we just listened to their truths. She said that the colors in the rainbow are always present to heal us and that every living thing has beautiful colors dancing throughout its being, making the world a glorious kaleidoscope.

She did not just *think* these beautiful thoughts. Our whole family was always doing some humanitarian project to benefit less fortunate people.

When I was five, we all worked at an Easter Seal Camp for crippled kids. My mother tells me that even then I would hold these kids in my lap. As I held one little girl with cerebral palsy, I could feel her muscle tension and spasms lessening. After a little while, she would gain enough control over her body to put on her braces.

I found out later than in Jin Shin there is an energy flow along the back of the legs which affects muscle tension and the skeletal structure. In some rudimentary form, I believe I was practicing Jin Shin without knowing it, even then.

So, when I got a phone call from my mother and sister back in 1973 and they told me about a class in Jin Shin which was being offered in Scottsdale, Arizona, I flew down from Denver and took it.

Mary Burmeister taught it. She is an American and the only person alive who studied with the Japanese master of the art, Jiro Murai. (This man, who died in the 1960s, dedicated his life to researching and practicing Jin Shin Jyutsu. His work is largely responsible for its revival in this century.) Mary's teachings have spread this art throughout the

United States and Europe. She has brought a great gift to the western world.

That class changed my life. I have always been people oriented, and Jin Shin gave me a process which allows me to interact with people and to see changes in their lives. So I decided to focus all my energy on practicing this art. Even though I've studied acupuncture, I can't "needle people." I do respect that form, but mine is a little different in that it focuses on the hands' energy.

What sort of philosophy underlies Jin Shin?

Behind Jin Shin and all the acupressure techniques is the belief that harmony and balance are the very essence of life. According to ancient Chinese philosophy, we experience disease and pain because of a poor balance between the yin and yang in our lives. The yin is defined as the feminine passive principle in nature that in Chinese cosmology is exhibited in darkness, cold, or wetness. The yang is the masculine active principle in nature that is exhibited in light, heat, or dryness. It combines with the yin to produce all that comes to be.

Balance is health. Health is balance. Our culture emphasizes the yang energy — the throwing yourself out, the driving of yourself.

The yin is often neglected in this country. It is more than sitting and being still. It is being receptive, becoming a vessel that can be filled, and then that vessel in turn is able to be very supportive and energetic.

Yin gives the energy to the yang to be expressed in some outward way. The space program is a dramatic example of the yang, thrusting out into space. It was interesting that on one mission an astronaut (Gerald Carr, *Skylab 4* mission) complained about being so task oriented that there was no time to reflect. He was feeling what happens when we don't replenish ourselves — if we don't cultivate the yin we become exhausted and out of balance.

What we have a chance at in this lifetime, basically, is to learn to recognize what is balance. We can learn when to give. When we are feeling empty, we can learn when to receive.

When we are out of balance, out of harmony, our bodies tell us very clearly. We have aches and pains. Or our emotions tell us. Relationships become negative. We become depressed. Jin Shin is one way to focus on *feeling* what is going on in our minds and bodies and to clear away anything that is blocking the balance in our lives.

Do you consider yourself a "healer?"

The way I see it, healing is done entirely by the person who comes in for treatment. I offer a form of counseling — hands on counseling. All I am is a catalyst. I try and bring into focus what the issues of energy blockage and imbalance are for each person. I support clients in taking a look at themselves and in releasing whatever imbalance or blockage they have.

Sometimes a client comes in knowing what the blockage is. Recently a woman came for a treatment who wanted help in leaving behind a painful part of her past. She and her husband had been through marriage therapy together, and although they were really happy together at this point she kept remembering some of the ways they had hurt each other before. She was having trouble forgetting.

We worked with giving her the energy to close the past. We did some mental imaging of packing the past away and locking it up. I worked on the energy flows connected with holding on to sadness and anger. (Jin Shin outlines specific energy flows tied to specific physical and emotional problems.)

She was able finally to release the past. In her case, one session provided this healing. But many times it is not this easy. We hold negative thought patterns because they meet some need in our lives. Even if that need is negative it is not that easy to turn loose.

How would you define a balanced person?

I would not even try. Each person is unique. Jin Shin does not impose any kind of structure of balancing on a person. It simply encourages each person to find his own.

I think that in our culture there is one widespread imbalance which afflicts many of us. If we could stop being so driven by outer appearances, we would be better balanced. We so often find an identity in our possessions. Our houses. Our cars. Our computers. Even our jobs become possessions when we give ourselves a certain value strictly by saying what we do and how much we make.

Eastern philosophies emphasize more who we are inside. Life is not just these outer forms. Of what value is a chair, really, until we sit down on it and our body and soul interact with it?

Could you summarize what happens in a treatment?

It is not easily "understandable," but a treatment is easy to experience. From the moment a person lies down, we begin to interact. As I touch the different pressure points, there is a nonverbal communication between us. There is a dance between our two energies.

By offering my energy to a place which is blocked — just as you would put jumper cables on a car — I support the client's energy flow. It's that simple.

The energy I offer comes through my fingers and it circulates very gently into various depths of the body as I touch someone. When my energy arrives at the place that is blocked, the person under treatment will borrow the energy long enough to build up enough power in his or her own flow to break the block or dam.

When I feel a pulsation in my fingers, I know that energy has been released and the blockage has been cleared. It is like an echo or "all clear" sign. When one path is cleared in this way, I move on to another that seems to be blocked.

Jin Shin is an art, not just a technique I'm applying. When two of us do it together, that person and I are creating an expression as artistic as a canvas or a dance. We are communing with God in a sense. It's uplifting. It's renewing.

How can I be sure that my relaxation and feeling of well-being come from unblocked energy flows rather than simply from your caring manner and gentle touch?

There is no extensive evidence yet, but I believe that modern science will allow us to prove all the things the healers knew thousands of years ago. The energy flows were documented two thousand years ago in a book called *The Emperor's Classic of Internal Medicine*. Recently there have been experiments for which electromagnetic-sensitive machines have been developed to study the validity of these energy healing arts. Amazingly, the energy flows can be seen, just as the book outlined them.

(Robert O. Becker, M.D., research professor and medical investigator at the Upstate Medical Centre, Syracuse, New York, is one of the most prominent researchers. In a paper written by Jin Shin Jyutsu practitioner

Ron Teeguarden, he comments on Becker's work, saying that it "supports the classical belief that a primitive energy system is at work in the living body, and that this system is not inherently reliant upon the gross structures of the body, including the nervous system.")

Note: Betsy Dayton now resides in Friday Harbor, Washington. She continues her practice there.

John Dunning: Life Outside the Tribe

The individual has always had to struggle to keep from being overwhelmed by the tribe. To be your own man is a hard business. If you try it, you will be lonely often and sometimes frightened. But no price is too high to pay for the privilege of owning yourself.

— Rudyard Kipling

If Denver novelist John Dunning did not agree with Kipling, he would not be home at 1 p.m. on a weekday, answering his doorbell clad in a sports shirt, casual navy slacks and matching socks, but no shoes.

"Come on in," he says, smiling broadly. "I've had a good workday," he adds, referring to his morning writing regimen. *Every* morning — weekends included — from 4 a.m. until around 10, Dunning writes.

John Dunning is a big, balding man with a slight belly rippling from the middle of his large frame. His muscular biceps crowd the short sleeves of his shirt, and he squints like one accustomed to driving into the sun for miles on end.

Passing through the neat living room of his modest frame house, he leads me down into his basement study. In his stocking feet he pads around his sanctum, showing it off with obvious pride. Floor-to-floor ceiling shelves hold close to one thousand books, including the five he has authored. Four are novels — *The Holland Suggestions, Looking for Ginger North, Denver,* and *Deadline*. The fifth is an encyclopedia about oldtime radio, *Tune in Yesterday.*

Dunning's office is orderly and packed with a novelist's tools and treasures. A sturdy old manual typewriter. Encyclopedias. Almanacs.

Files. Smiling photographs taken some years before of his son Jim and daughter Katie.

Dunning retreated to this cozy, carpeted room after running away from the "tribe," which he defines at first only as "an awful thing." Later in our conversation, he is more specific. In his estimation, the tribe is the organized work force — companies, corporations, and even smaller enterprises — which force employees to adhere to *their* priorities and schedules at the expense of individual creativity and initiative.

Of necessity, Dunning performed tribal rituals for a long time. After dropping out of tenth grade back in Charleston, South Carolina, he worked as a glass cutter. Later he headed west to Colorado and worked as a groom at Centennial Race Track in Littleton. Finally, in 1966, he landed a job as a library clerk at the *Denver Post*, and in 1967 he moved into a reporter's slot.

It's not that he did not appreciate that reporting job. But making up his own tales, not tracking down stories assigned to him, is what he wanted to do. In short, he felt stifled. So in 1970 he quit. Except for a brief stint back at the *Post* in 1974, he has stayed far from smoke-filled city rooms and the stress of rush-hour traffic ever since.

Dunning's determination alone did not earn him the peace and quiet he finds in his study in south suburban Denver. His wife, Helen, a former social worker, now a secretary, computer operator, and administrative assistant at Reproductive Genetics Center, has been an integral part of his ability to work at home. During the lean years before he had a New York agent and a stack of books between covers, she underwrote his dreams.

Now with book royalties, with a once-a-week spot on KNUS radio in Denver hosting the "Old Time Radio Show," with teaching writing courses at Metro State College, and most recently, with the opening of the Old Algonquin Bookstore on East Colfax in Denver, Dunning has put together a collage of nontribal pursuits which, when coupled with Helen's salary, support the family well enough. (Dunning earned a high school equivalency certificate and took some college courses but never finished. Apparently, *teaching* in college is more to his liking.)

Dunning believes, as Kipling did, that "no price is too high to pay for the privilege of owning yourself." In his case, the price is not knowing exactly how he'll put the kids through college or make next year's mortgage payments.

But would he return to the tribe? "Hell no," says the usually gentle man when prodded into talking about a subject about which he feels anything but mild mannered. . . .

Conversations

Why do you want to be on your own so badly?

I have found that I can't work for any organization big enough to have an employment director — or a staff of idiots who control the day-to-day flow of what you do. Their job, in fact, seems to be to stifle creativity, to sit on it, and to trample it down.

I've seen so many of my friends, reporters who, after spending their lives in those places, by the age of fifty don't have anything left. Many of these guys obviously had a spark of some kind when they were young. I've run across stories old-time reporters did that I wouldn't have thought them capable of doing, because they seem so *old* now, and they've been in the system for so long. Yet at one time, they were young, and they were energetic, and they dug for stories. The tribe discourages individual creative excellence.

Where does your independence come from?

As a young man, I worked in a glass factory in South Carolina. Even then I was saying to myself, my God, how do I get out of this? I was making $1.50 an hour; guys who stayed twenty to twenty-five years made $2.25 an hour. That was their idea of the big time. There's got to be more to life, I thought to myself.

I go back and walk through that glass shop now, and I have friends who are still there. And they're twenty years older, and they're still bitching about their jobs. I remember always coming in mornings and dreading the day ahead of me. It was one of absolute tedium and boring busywork.

When I worked there we had a wit named Andy Catterton. We used a lot of aluminum for making storefront window frames, and Andy would make himself stuff and take it home. The boss came by one time and said, "Andy, what are you making?"

Andy was standing there holding a mailbox. With a deadpan expression, he just answered, "A dollar and a half an hour, sir."

Andy's still there. . . .

But you still have to deal with the tribe, don't you, even as a novelist?

Yes. I *wish* I could stay the hell away from the tribe, and I *wish* my books would get published by some magical process that has nothing to do with dollars and cents. If I could make enough money to keep my little world here, without dealing with publishers, I would. All I want is to educate my kids, keep myself and my wife happy, keep myself in tape and books. But to preserve this existence, I do still have to interact with the tribe on occasion.

It must be incredibly hard to discipline yourself to work at home. How do you do it?

At first it *was* hard. I had the mistaken idea that if I quit my job to work on a novel, then I would work on a novel. But I quit work and soon found that my days were eaten up with other things. I would work in political campaigns. I worked for Craig Barnes.I worked for Dale Tooley. I worked for Pat Schroeder. This was important work, but I wasn't getting any writing done.

Finally, I decided that the only thing to do was to find a time during the day when the phone doesn't ring, because if somebody calls up and says, "Let's go have a beer," I'll go. I'd lots rather drink beer than write. I don't even *like* beer, so that says something about the pain of writing. I'd rather *talk* about writing. That's much more fun.

The first week of getting up at 4 a.m. was sheer hell. And then it got easier. It got to be just what I did. I had to start going to bed at 9 though.

Somebody once asked me, "What do you do if you want to stay out late the night before?" I don't. I go to bed, and I get up and work on my book. Very, very occasionally I will cop out.

I write every day. Saturday, Sunday, Allegheny River Day. I don't care what day it is, I get up and do my stuff. Christmas, New Year's, even on holidays, I'll work at least those few hours in the morning before breakfast.

If you get up at four in the morning and you don't write, you feel really stupid. So you sit down with a blank piece of paper and you say, I'm going to write something even if it's bad. After awhile you learn that all first drafts are bad. And you learn how to cope with your own awfulness.

Do you have trouble stopping?

No. I love to stop. Writing is an extremely painful process to me, because it is not fun. It's enormously satisfying, but it is not fun. When I am satisfied that I have done a decent day's work, then I will quit. I will quit right in the middle of a sentence. I'll quit in the middle of a love scene. That's the best time to quit, because if the characters are in bed, and you've got all your juices worked up, then all it takes is sitting down at that typewriter and retyping that last half page the next day.

Now if you'd let them culminate the love scene, or if you had not even started it — well, pardon my crudity, but you'd have to get it up all over again.

How much of you is in the characters in your novels?

I'm in all of them. Too much. I'm Tom Hastings in *Denver* (his novel about the Ku Klux Klan in Denver in the 1920s). I'm also Walker in *Deadline*. In the books, they do what I would love to do. They go in and tell the managing editor off. And, because they're such great reporters, they get away with it. We all would like to tell the managing editor off, because managing editors deserve to be told off.

Why did you go back briefly to the Denver Post *as a reporter in 1974?*

I went back out of necessity. We had a new baby. We needed the money. I told myself I'd work on my next novel after work, but I would come home too drained.

Finally, my agent sold *The Holland Suggestions*, and I got an advance from the publisher. It was only $2,500, but I saw I could begin to earn something from my writing.

From all outward appearances, things were going great with my reporting. I was getting front-page stories. They were turning me loose to dig up stories on my own. But, as often as not, I'd sneak out at two or three in the afternoon, and drift around and go bar hopping with some of the guys. That's a sure road to death . . . I'm talking about spiritual death. I knew I had to quit, and so one day I came home and said to Helen, "What do you say we both quit?"

At that point Helen was burnt out with social work, too. We bit the bullet, and both of us quit our jobs in the same week. Helen was off about two years. I went back to my writing. We had saved enough to make it through, to pay our bills.

When Helen went back to work, she and another caseworker managed to talk Denver Welfare into letting them split a job, something that had never been done before. There was a lot of flap over it. They didn't want to do it because it was too creative, because it might make them too fresh and less burnt-out on their jobs. (He says this sarcastically, then laughs.)

So, Helen was able to work just two and a half days a week. That satisfies her need to not be so tied down to the household. And her steady paycheck meant that I did not have to pound the boards.

Do you find that people envy you, thinking that your life must be much simpler and easier than theirs?

Down in their hearts, they know it's not easy. Because if they really thought it was easy, they'd do it, too. You encounter a lot of jealousy. I don't have much patience with that stuff.

A friend of mine, Jack Kisling, told me once that he overheard two reporters talking at the Press Club, and one said to the other, "Wouldn't it be nice to be able to live the way Dunning lives?" I just looked at Jack and said, "These guys haven't got the faintest idea how I live."

But they have a fantasy of what your life is like?

Yes. But you see, the thing is, they don't understand what the price is. The price is kind of an empty loneliness, like Kipling said. You're by yourself a lot.

I've learned not only to deal with that, but to really enjoy it. I enjoy the daytimes when Helen and the kids are gone. I can get a lot of work done. And then when they do come home, I can enjoy that, too.

Do you and Helen divide the chores?

We don't get clinical about it. But I cook four suppers a week usually.

I'm responsible for the basement — my study and den. When we have company, I vacuum and straighten down here. She does the upstairs. Helen cooks for company, because she's better at that than I am. I just have five or six basic meals that I cook. They're "home" meals.

A lot of men cook only for company, like chefs for show. . . .

Not me! But Helen does get stuck with more of the day-in and day-out kids' activities, like meetings and conferences at school. They keep giving the kids half days off, and they don't seem to think much about working parents. They love to send a note home with the kids one night, assigning you a time to come and meet with them. They expect you to show up. They just say, "Your meeting is scheduled for 10 o'clock on Thursday," and you have to take time off from work. Usually they want to see you for fifteen minutes.

Last week one of these was coming up. Since Helen would have had to drive all the way home from work, I just started my writing earlier in the morning that day.

We like to spend a lot of time with our kids. Last summer Helen was in between jobs. I would get up even earlier to write, and by the middle of the morning, we would leave to take the kids bowling or to go up to the mountains or some kind of outing.

One thing is certain, the kids know me. They may not always like me. But they know me.

What are you working on now?

I'm just finishing a novel — a 950-page book about my hometown, Charleston, South Carolina, during the Civil War. Charleston had the longest siege in the history of this country — five hundred and some odd days. It culminated in a place called Battery Wagner. It was an epic struggle, and it's been almost forgotten because it happened at the same time Gettysburg and Vicksburg were going on. For four years, I've been working on this novel — for better or worse, it'll be ready to go late this year.

Do you go through discouraging, "down" times during such long writing projects?

Yes. And when I'm down I make Helen and the kids miserable. I may get angry with her and she gets mad because she doesn't understand what I want. She'll come home from work and we'll sit down and I'll start to talk about something, and suddenly she'll look past me and start talking to the kids. I know *why* she's distracted, but sometimes I just turn and storm out. And then I come down here and turn on my tapes.

Luckily, I don't do too much of that. When I am down, though, I am *all* the way down. Like many writers I know — the highs are so high, but the lows. . . .

But, that's the stuff of living.

But it's worth it?

I wouldn't trade places with anybody. I've got a great wife and great kids. I've got a room full of books and a hobby that has become a semi-vocation. (He collects old radio shows on tape and uses them on his Sunday radio show.)

What else do I need? I'd like to make a little more from my writing. I'd rather be able to enjoy all of this without wondering *how* I can keep going financially. But I'd rather be worrying about how to keep it going than to have to live like everybody else has to live. You just don't get another chance at life. . . .

There isn't a newspaper in the country that could hire me today, and that's no jive. I've found that the closer you get to the big time, the smaller it looks. I don't give a damn about money, except in the sense that I wish I had some of it. But I don't want it enough to make the sacrifices that I'd have to make to get it.

Randy Gradishar: Tackling a New Career

If Randy Gradishar were accidentally to trip someone on a crowded sidewalk, he would undoubtedly bend over to help the person up, apologize profusely, and insist on giving him a ride home. Never mind that this big, amiable ex-Denver Bronco linebacker used to tackle people for a living. That was different. His reputation both on and off the field has always been that of a courteous, good-natured gentleman.

Drafted by the Broncos immediately after graduating from Ohio State University in 1974, Gradishar played for ten consecutive seasons with the team, never missing a game. He appeared in seven Pro Bowls and was voted either All-NFL or All-AFC linebacker seven consecutive seasons. By the time he retired at age thirty-one in 1983, he had posted 2,049 tackles in his career, the highest published total in pro football over that past decade.

Gradishar grew up in the small northeastern Ohio community of Champion and met his wife Janet there. "We started dating in high school," he recalls. "My father had a grocery store on one corner, and her father had a Dairy Queen on the other. I would go over for lunch breaks and she would give me free milkshakes. After two summers, I knew I'd eventually marry this girl!" They were married in 1973 and now have three children: Paige, Meredith, and Mark.

After his retirement from football, Gradishar became president of the Denver Broncos Youth Foundation, which is located in the Denver Bronco headquarters. His office there holds photos of his family and a few mementos from his football career. On a coffee table is a small book, *What Kids Need Most in a Dad*. In an ornate frame on one wall is a piece of almost burnt toast with the inscription below it, "A Toast to Randy for His Retirement."

"That piece of toast was from my friends," he says. "Janet held a retirement party for me and they presented me with that."

Gradishar did not decide overnight to retire from football and to enter a new career. While we sit at a small, round table in one corner of his office, he talks about these changes, his Christian faith, and his commitment to Janet and his children.

He rests his large hands on the table and periodically picks up a pencil and gestures with it, pointing emphatically while he talks. I expect to encounter some latent middle-linebacker aggressiveness or to glimpse evidence of a large ego deflated by the loss of the adulation of fanatical Bronco fans. Instead, he relates his story with the simple sincerity of a minister or a priest.

Conversations

Why did you choose to retire when you did?

I wanted to be in the best physical condition I could when I left football. I didn't want to leave because an injury forced me out. Sometimes players are cut. Sometimes they are traded. I feel very blessed that I was with the Broncos for ten years.

I also wanted to leave the game at my peak. In my mind, if I had played any longer, I felt I might begin to cheat the team and myself. It wasn't an easy decision. There was a lot of time spent thinking about it. There was a lot of prayer involved.

So you were prepared for this retirement?

Yes. Even that first season I knew that football was only going to last for so long. I was already thinking, some day you'll be out of football, and then what are you going to do?

My parents taught me the work ethic, so it seemed natural to work in the off-season (from February to June). I didn't just lie around at home and take it easy. I took various jobs that would give me some practical experience.

During my first four off-seasons, I worked at Adolph Coors Brewery in Golden. Since I was practically raised in my father's grocery store and since I had worked in a sporting goods store during summers, I had picked up some experience in retail business. At Coors, I worked in sales and marketing. Later, I got involved in a residential burglar alarm business. All my off-season jobs were retail-sales oriented.

About halfway through my football career, I started thinking that there must be something I would be more interested in doing with my life than those off-season jobs. Profit and loss statements — five-year projection sheets — I had to admit they just didn't excite me.

All along, I was talking out things with my wife. Janet didn't make my decision to retire, but she had a great deal of input. Because football is such a big part of both of our lives,she knew well what I was going through in trying to decide when to quit and what to do after I retired. (Janet taught for five years before their first daughter was born in 1977.)

In my eighth season with the Broncos, someone recommended that I read a career planning book, *What Color Is Your Parachute?*. It asks you to write down what you think you want to do, why you want to do it, where you want to work, how much money you want to make — those kinds of things. Then, after doing these exercises, I found out about a career planning company in Connecticut called People's Management, a Christian-oriented company that deals with executives or anybody in business who wants to make a career change.

I wasn't able to attend their seminars, but I filled out all their long questionnaires and they sent back a vocational assessment of me. They found that my motivational thrust is "to shape, lead, and influence people." And they advised me that I would do well in a serving, civic-minded atmosphere. Their findings affirmed that my aptitudes and interests did not fit into a sales or marketing career.

And this helped you decide to accept your current position?

Yes. When Edgar Kaiser (ex-owner of the Denver Broncos who formed the Denver Broncos Youth Foundation in 1982) asked me to head up the foundation, I was excited about the opportunity to help young people.

What we hope to do is to help young people with their physical, emotional, mental, and spiritual needs. We will serve as a catalyst among existing organizations that work with youth — not just with handicapped programs or with drug and alcohol abuse programs or with Christian youth groups, but with all kinds of youth organizations — Boy Scouts, Future Farmers of America. We're hoping to help these groups coordinate programs and work together. We're setting goals and developing strategies now. We're assessing carefully just how we can best serve young people.

Has the transition from football to the foundation been hard?

It's not been the easiest in the world. Because I knew the timing was right, I didn't sit around and ask myself, "Geez, why did you do this?" But I did have some emotional feelings, especially when the Broncos played the first regular season game back in September (1984). It's not that I miss playing so much, but after doing it seventeen years in a row, there was an emotional letdown.

Still, because I'm such a "plan ahead" type of person, my retirement and all the changes it made in my life did not take me by surprise. Sometimes, I tend to go overboard in being so systematic about things. My wife says, "Why don't you just make a decision?"

Well, I'm not intuitive like she is. If there are ten steps in a process, I have to do all ten. My wife can do the first three and sense what she should do next.

But, as I've explained, I had to read books. I had to fill out questionnaires. I had to talk to ex-football players like my friends Merlin Olsen (former Rams player, now a sports announcer) and his brother Phil Olsen (who played with the Rams and Broncos).

Janet and I had counseling together where we took some personality tests. Now I think she understands that I *have* to be this methodical. I understand better that she can make decisions without going into all this detail. We're accepting each other's different approaches.

You seem content now . . .

Yes . . . My Christian faith has held me together more than anything else. My favorite verse in the Bible is "and whatsoever ye do, do it heartily, as to the Lord, and not unto men . . ." (from Colossians 3:23, King James translation). Sometimes I will lose my focus, but my goal is to work for the Lord and not for man. And that means I don't need other people's approval so much as I need just to do my best. I don't need to worry myself about comparing myself with anybody else. I think that tends to make for contentment.

When I was playing football, I was always compared to other linebackers—Jack Lambert of the Pittsburgh Steelers—Dick Butkus of the Chicago Bears. When reporters would ask me, "How are you different?" I would answer, "You guys can figure that out. I'm just doing what *I* can do."

When I talk to kids I say, "Don't worry about comparing yourself to others. Don't worry about stacking up to somebody else. Do what you can do, and if you can only run so fast, you can only run so fast. If you can only read so fast, you can only read so fast."

I would have pursued a business degree at Ohio State, but I was not that smart in math. So I majored in education with an emphasis that gave me some of the same marketing and accounting courses I would have taken with a business major. I had to face that I couldn't handle statistics courses and other higher math courses. We all have gifts and talents . . . to be able just to look inwardly and do everything we can means we don't have to compare ourselves with others.

How do you keep such a strong faith?

It's a daily thing. I relate keeping it to staying fit and competent as an athlete. To be a professional football player or a college or high school athlete, you must train. Run. Sweat. Get injured. Sacrifice. Well, that kind of dedication, plus more, is needed in a Christian commitment.

I'm not saying I have all that, but that's what I try to attain. Sometimes I get my priorities mixed up, but I keep going back to the Bible and seeing that it emphasizes faith and love and service to others. It calls for commitment to Jesus and dedication to all he taught.

In our society, success is measured by the money you make — what you can buy. I believe success is measured in how you use the gifts and talents God has given you. Success is not winning football games or buying cars or houses.

What are your priorities right now?

My relationship with God is first, then my family, then friends, then my job. I think it's easy to fall into wanting to be the best athlete, to be the best company president or the best plumber or farmer. We spend so much time and effort working toward success that we neglect or sacrifice something if we are not careful. Anyone who puts a career first — a man or a woman who chooses the fast track — will most often neglect his or her family ties.

What do you hope you will have accomplished when you look back at your life in years to come?

If I can look back and say that my marriage was happy and my children were brought up so that they felt good about themselves and had integrity and honesty — if I can know that I've exerted a Christian influence on them and helped lead them to a belief in Christ — then I could care less about all the other things.

If I'm out trying to help other kids and youth leaders and I don't have my own home and my relationships there intact, then I'm just fooling myself and being a hypocrite. I have to be successful at home first. Then I can look at being successful outside my home.

Keeping priorities straight is a continuing process. We all struggle. Janet and I struggle like everybody else. If somebody says they don't have any struggles, that they're going down "easy street," I don't believe them.

The reality is that relationships, especially family relationships, take a lot of work. There has to be a commitment and a willingness to work through problems. There are no guarantees in this life, but if I can keep my commitment to my faith and my family, I think I'll have the energy to do my best at work, too.

So you don't just appear occasionally at home to give your wife and children "quality" time?

No! Do you think the people you are close to are thrilled with "quality" time? How would you feel if you went into a restaurant and said, "Give me the best steak you've got," and the waiter came back and served you a tiny little piece. So you tell the waiter you're starving! "That's the best quality — the best little filet we have!" he says. And you say, "But I'm not into quality that much. I need some *quantity*!" The whole quality-quantity stuff, in my opinion, is for the birds.

Kids don't want the biggest toys, the nicest clothes. They want you to get down and play with them. Really, they just want your time, for you to be available. But it's easier to say, "I'll buy them this' and they'll be happy."

It takes a lot of time to build trust with kids. If you take the time, it will develop.

Do you think you'll always be the kind of person who plans ahead?

That won't change. I'm already thinking, soon I'll have teenagers. Then they'll be off to college or to work. Then my wife and I are going to be on our own again. What interests will I keep? Which ones will change? How long will I work?

I like to look forward like this. It's hard for me to undersand that all of a sudden I could get to sixty-five and not know what I would do. I'll know, if I live that long, because I will have "pre-thought" about it.

All this planning involves Janet. I need to stay in touch with what she's wanting our life to be in the future. If I were to plan and she were to plan, but we never consulted each other — we might find ourselves going in opposite directions. So we try and keep communicating.

And your faith keeps you trying to live each day with your priorities and goals in mind?

Yes. Most days I see a lot of mistakes in myself. I guess I would not need my faith if I were perfect. There is a Psalm which says, "This is the day which the Lord has made; let us rejoice and be glad in it" (Psalm 118:24, Revised Standard Version).

It's all too easy to hang onto our pasts, but after each day is over, it's history. If we did something right, or even something spectacular that brought us some recognition or fame, that's over. If we goofed, if we *failed* in some outstanding way, that's over.

Each day is a new day. Faith has to stay in the present tense. Football was just a part of my life. It's pleasant to look back on the Superbowls, all those things — but I try hard and focus on the present.

(Randy Gradishar continues to serve as president of the Denver Broncos Youth Foundation. For more information about this program, write the Denver Broncos Youth Foundation, 5700 Logan Street, Denver, CO 80216.)

Joanne Greenberg: The Laws That Order One Writer's Life

Appropriately, Joanne Greenberg, author of the bestselling novel *I Never Promised You a Rose Garden*, cultivates no roses outside her Lookout Mountain home west of Denver. Instead she tends the white lilacs and cherry trees that grow there among native wild flowers, lodgepole pines, and aspens.

Though lilac bushes and cherry trees are not supposed to survive the Rockies' capricious climate, they thrive here nevertheless. Greenberg, a transplanted Easterner born and raised in New York City, flourishes in this setting, too. She is one of a small percentage of fiction writers nationwide who is able to make a living just by writing.

Twenty-eight years ago, she and her husband Albert, a retired psychotherapist, built their compact, contemporary house. In the meadow that wraps around the front and sides of the moss rock and cedar home, several neatly stacked piles of wood await next winter. Out back, the land falls away steeply to an airy panorama of the Front Range. In the valley far below, Interstate 70, flecked with matchbox-sized cars, twists like two grey chords.

In this setting, the Greenbergs have raised two sons, Alan and David, now grown, and here Joanne does her writing. "I write every morning from seven to eight-thirty, not at a desk, but" — she points to the master bedroom off the living room — "in there, on my side of the bed. I came to writing fiction through poetry, and that means you write by the word," she says, explaining her short work day. "A journalist uses a typewriter or a word processor. I use pencil and paper. I concentrate as hard as I can during that hour and a half, and after that I've had it." Keeping this morning ritual, she has completed nine novels and three collections of short stories.

In such prestigious publications as the *New York Times* and *Time Magazine*, critics keep praising Greenberg's work. Fans — a large band of them — continue to devour each new offering, yet strangers still meet her and say, "I read your book. Have you written any others?" They are referring, of course, to *Rose Garden* (her abbreviation of the longer title), published in 1964 and made into a movie in 1978. To date, close to seven million books have been sold, earning her both the income and reputation to continue writing fiction.

Since Greenberg is not inclined to brag about all this, some locals are not aware that she is an author. More visible to them are her other involvements. For over twenty years, armed with lively and often obscure information about the English language, she has taught etymology to sixth graders at Ralston Elementary School on Lookout Mountain. She teaches Hebrew to children in her Jewish congregation and occasionally lectures at Jefferson County Open High School in Evergreen, Colorado. Besides these volunteer posts, she recently began teaching a course in anthropology at Colorado School of Mines in Golden. A graduate of the American University in Washington, D.C., Greenberg majored in anthropology.

For twelve years she has worked as a volunteer fire fighter at the Lookout Mountain Fire Department. Until last year she worked as an emergency medical technician for the Highland Volunteer Rescue Squad.

While others obviously are impressed with her devotion to community service and with her literary achievements, Greenberg is not. When introduced as a "local treasure" to the audience at a benefit for the Evergreen library, her response was a skeptical, "Oh God — are they talking about me?"

"I never do anything that isn't fun," she insists. "I don't believe in that. If I were really into self-sacrifice, I'd be on some kind of board where they have a lot of meetings," she says with a laugh.

Greenberg, whose fire-fighting equipment — ropes, a hatchet, and a pick — hangs from sturdy hooks by the front door, does not decorate either her home or herself with anything not functional. She wears jeans and sturdy sandals. Now in her early fifties, her hair is a soft grey, cut into a short haircut that encircles her face and falls into bangs just above round pastel blue-framed glasses. She is a tall woman — solid and strong, but soft and feminine, too.

While applying elaborate makeup or camouflaging the grey in her hair has little appeal to Greenberg, making up tales from an apparently limitless imagination does. The *Denver Post* calls her "a remarkable writer who shows the light and dark places of human souls." She calls herself a storyteller (or "liar" in more candid moments), not a philosopher. But what if by telling a story a truth is illustrated? "Of course, you hope that happens," she says.

Though spinning a good tale is her first concern, in all her writing, moral and religious themes are either exposed openly or hidden in some allegory or metaphor. For instance, in *Founder's Praise* (1976) she traces the birth and death of a religious cult on the Colorado plains. In *The Far Side of Victory* (1983), set in a small Colorado mountain town, she explores issues of justice, love, and loss in a chilling tale about a reckless young driver, Eric Arnold Gordon.

Sometimes religious themes reflect Greenberg's own deep Judaic faith. In her only historical novel, *The King's Persons* (1963), she writes about a massacre of Jews in England near the end of the twelfth century. In *A Season of Delight* (1981), the novel's main character, like Greenberg herself, is a middle-aged woman who works on the local emergency squad and who observes Judaic holidays and traditions.

Many of her short stories are peopled with Jewish characters. In her most recent collection, *High Crimes and Misdemeanors*, Aunt Bessie, in the story "Certain Distant Suns," is a woman who stops believing in God and even in gravity, and who ends up bobbing around on the ceiling, weightless.

Unlike her fictional Aunt Bessie, the keeping of her faith is crucial to Greenberg. On a chain around her neck, she wears a single ornament, a mezuzah, symbol and reminder that the laws and concepts of her religion are to be lived each day. How her faith is woven into her life and work — what that means to her — is the theme of the following conversation.

Greenberg comments first on her most famous book and talks about the struggle it depicts. *Rose Garden*, a fictionalized account of Greenberg's real teenage fight with mental illness, relates the story of a sixteen-year-old girl's retreat from reality into a mad, imaginary kingdom. Happily, like another of her titles, Greenberg is on the far side of that victory.

Conversations

Is Rose Garden *actually as religious a book as some of your others? Was Deborah's (the protagonist's) madness a substitute for religion?*

In reviewing the book, nobody has dealt with this. I wonder why, because I think if nonreligious people — if Madeleine O'Hair (the outspoken atheist) read *Rose Garden* and then read some of my other books, she would say, "Well, Greenberg just went from one craziness to another." But the *Rose Garden* gods were actually a kind of self-mocking parody of Jewish religious life.

In *Rose Garden* there is another language. There are special words and special customs and special deeds — the whole world of special words and special requirements and requests, just as there are in Judaism.

If the basis of all parody is admiration, which I think it is, then you understand what happened. The kingdom Deborah invented was less the mad part than it was a kind of creative expression from somebody who was locked into this prison fort (of madness).

At the end of the book, Deborah's transition from madness to health was tremendously difficult for her. In reality, how hard was it for you?

It was very hard, but once I made that commitment, there was a terrific amount of excitement, a terrific amount of hunger that had been bottled up for a long, long time. The book is only partly autobiographical. I was sicker for a lot longer than the book talks about. But I think there was a backup of healthy enthusiasm and teenage vitality in me that helped a lot.

I had a very good therapist. Also, probably one of the best things that happened to me isn't allowed anymore. I was in a mental hospital that housed both men and women of all ages. Now, there's a *teen* ward, a *pre-teen* ward, and *post-teen* ward. There are all kinds of psychological reasons for segregating people this way and I think it's bird lime. I think it's sheep dip. Because I learned by living with those adults — just seeing them. I knew that *if* I lived, I would soon be an adult. They helped teach me what this meant.

Do you think your illness gave you a greater appreciation for "right now?"

I don't think there is anyone who ever crawled, recovered, out of a mental facility who doesn't have that appreciation. Your therapist, your doctor . . . nobody ever tells you that this appreciation is going to be an unearned "extra." And it sounds so cliche. Some days do go by when I'm not thankful, when I've forgotten. But underneath I always keep this appreciation. This is the only tie I still have with my sickness. I used to have a kind of arrogance and superiority about dealing with mentally ill people just because I had been mentally ill.

I relinquished that on a call in the ambulance while I was working as an emergency medical technician. That day I said to the other technician, "I'm not getting anywhere with this disturbed woman. I think you can do better," and she did.

Before I had felt "this is one of mine." That day I understood that when you get well enough, you don't do any better than anyone else. It was one of my finest hours.

So this tie to the mentally ill is not relevant anymore. Are you tied to orthodox Judaism?

No. I call those Jews who keep all the laws, the "real" Jews. To them I'm not a Jew at all. We don't keep a kosher home. *Season of Delight* yielded letters from women who were very angry at me for what they considered the slackness of my personal religious orthodoxy. But the part of Judaism that I do have and use is mine and it is quite orthodox.

In the short story "Certain Distant Suns" (from High Crimes and Misdemeanors*) you write, "Foolish woman, a soul goes in and out of belief a hundred times a day. Belief is too fragile to weigh a minute on." Is your belief fragile?*

Yes, I'm a rope dancer in my faith. For instance, I believe in my marriage, but Albert and I caught the whooping cough in Pennsylvania not long ago. For weeks we were busy giving concerts to each other all night long. And when you're in the middle of that, you feel like saying, "Why don't you shut up?"

But even when I was thinking this I knew, "I love this guy, but I wish he'd go away."

And you want to say that to the Lord. That may happen a dozen times a day. We need to be aware of our limitations. Because our own feelings fluctuate so much, this is why we need the law. We're not strong enough to weigh good and evil.

Is there a law for everything in Judaism?

Everything. In orthodox Judaism, almost every move you make is for the purpose of being conscious of all your acts, always.

For instance, what shoe goes on first. Is it *sock*, then *shoe*? Or is it *sock, sock — shoe, shoe*? The purpose of such a law is to make us conscious of what we're doing *all the time*. And hopefully, we are grateful all the time.

Now people laugh at this kind of thing, and they laugh like hell, and it *is* funny. There is so much that is *legislated, legislated, and legislated*. A person who's grown up in a modern society may want to run screaming out the door just thinking of all these laws, but the paradox is this — I see people who would die if they had to follow Jewish law. Yet their "kashrut," their legalism, is politics or feminism.

For example, feminists make minute, hair-splitting differences in language usage. Does it really matter if I say "salesgirl, salesperson, or saleswoman?" Is it terrible if someone calls me a "lady" instead of a "woman?"

So all these laws are to make one constantly conscious of every act, every thought — but not to make a religion of the law itself?

Behind this is the principle that you ought to have certain "hevdels" — or separations, in your life. Hevdel is a big word in Judaism. It means discrimination and separation. It separates sacred from profane, and it separates day from night.

Havdalah, which ends the Sabbath, is a Jewish ceremony I particularly like. In it we thank God for the ability to discriminate between light and darkness, between a stench and a fragrance. The poorest person can do that. And when you think about it, that's a tremendous privilege.

Why did nature, or providence, give us ten thousand odors? It's not necessary — God threw it in. Biosociologists say that in order to stay alive we need just the ability to smell three odors — burning, rotten, and pheromones.

It's not necessary that we see color either. To discriminate subtly the differences between one color and another is not going to make us better hunters or even better gatherers. The ceremony of havdalah obliges us to remember that.

But you do not always keep each and every law, do you?

No. Any law *can, shall, must* be shattered when good sense tells you that the law is not compassionate. There has to be a war between situational ethics and frozen ethics. (She spreads open her right hand, palm up.) If my hand is still, it's only because the tug on this side (she points to her thumb) is equal to the tug on that side (she touches her little finger). This stillness is possible only in the midst of continuously contending forces.

I have a somewhat mystical turn of mind, and when Jews are mystics, we are mystics in an extremely anti-mystical tradition. Again, there is a nice fight in mysticism, a tension I love. We have the freedom of a balloon which is really never allowed to float free. For example, a mystic runs in and says to a rabbi, "I've had a revelation from the Lord. I just heard from the Lord, and He said, 'Arise and go forth.' " (In other words, the mystic has received a directive from God to do something specific, something not contained within the law.)

The rabbi says, "I noticed you rushed in and your old Father is sitting over there. It says in the Talmud you should always greet your Father. You should ask after his health and see that he's all right."

"I know this," the mystic answers, "but I'm excited about this revelation. Listen, please — the Lord said to me —"

The rabbi interrupts. "*You* listen. Did you feed your cat first thing in the morning?" (According to Talmudic law, animals must be fed first.)

"Did you tend to the cat?" the rabbi asks insistently.

"Yeah, yeah," the mystic answers, "I did. But won't you listen? I'm trying to tell you something about a revelation from the Lord!"

"Yes, I know," the rabbi answers, "but did you wash your hands when you got up this morning? You can get sick if you don't do that."

By the time the mystic got to his revelation, it would be forgotten. Revelation in Judaism is always fought down by the minutae. I think that's especially hard when you're growing up. Young people want that revelation. They want to have that bright light. But instead, the rabbi is always bringing us down to this mundane level of dailiness.

But when you are in middle life, as I am now, something happens. You finally understand that it's the pinheads of daily life that accrue to make the mountain you're going to stand on to get closer to God. There *is* a place for revelation, but reality is more the day-in and day-out observance of the law. You do a little better this day. You help someone fix this. You do that . . . .

When my boys were growing up I told them, "You pay no dues, you get no benefits."

In the 1960s, people were asking, "Does life have a meaning?" My answer's got to be — probably not. *Putting* a meaning into life is always a "do-it-yourself" job.

What Jewish observations have added meaning to your life?

The Sabbath — it's the observance the Jews gave to the world. Back in Roman days people worked seven days a week. But this pokey little tribe of Jews who never numbered any more than thirty thousand back then — living in one of the worst deserts on the face of the earth — they had this idea that man is not an animal, that the least person has a right to contemplate the heavens, as much right as the greatest philosopher. So, on the Sabbath, everybody quits working, by law.

Keeping the Sabbath saved my marriage. I sound like something in *True Confessions*, but it's true. When we were building this house and the kids were small, it would have been easy to shove aside the Sabbath, to shove aside God. But once a week, then and now, everybody sits down and cools off, quiets down, and appreciates what a home life is. *By law.* Without that law, it's too easy to say, "Well, next week . . ."

We all wonder at times if keeping a law like this is worth it. The world with all its variety is out there, and God knows it's more charming than the same old laws and routines.

Speaking of routine — I hear you still do your own ironing, your own cooking, and housework. Isn't it tempting to stop doing some of this?

Isn't that everybody's romance? To get out of daily details? Oh, but we always say, "If I only had a maid to take care of this . . ."

I hate the clutter. (She glances around her living room. Several pairs of slacks she has ironed hang on a hook next to the fireplace, on their way to the bedroom. A pair of hiking boots rests on the hearth.)

Why doesn't somebody pick that up? (She points to a newspaper on the end table.) Not me. *Somebody*. I could then come home to this serenity. I could waft in and out and I could save myself for better things, higher things. (She laughs heartily.)

Talmudic law says you're supposed to work, and Talmudic law has yet to toss me a raspberry. You're *supposed* to sweat. You're *supposed* to pick up after yourself. All these little things harness you to sanity. They harness you to reality.

Are there any laws in your writing?

In fact, yes. And in many ways, this is a women's issue. There are always more important things to do than your writing. The excuses are the easiest things, especially women's excuses — "I don't have the money. I'm taking care of my poor old mother . . ." Well, your poor old mother can wait an hour. What has to happen so that you do not use these excuses is to make your writing a law issue.

The Jewish law says that terrible things will happen if you don't keep the law. And the law in my writing says, "The pencils shall have been sharpened previous to the beginning of the writing session. The paper shall have to have been supplied previous to the beginning of the session."

That is number one and number two. Number three? There is a choice — one single choice per writing session. Either I work or I sit and stare at the paper. So, I don't read a little and then go back. I don't "bop-she-bop-she" here and there. If you don't have a law about it, you don't do it.

In Season of Delight, *Grace, the main character, says, "If the highways and the heart attacks and the booze and the bridge abutments gave me a thousand a day to rescue, I couldn't make up one of the cities of my lost people in a lifetime." Are you, like Grace, trying to make up for some of the terrible loss of the Holocaust by doing your fire and rescue work?*

Yes, but the argument is that if you worked all day and all night forever — if you saved a person an hour, you couldn't make up that loss in fifty years.

But that shouldn't stop us. I really do believe, too, that the people who died in the Holocaust used up the sufferings of their life, but that they didn't use up the joy. There's a whole lot of unlived joy — joy that has to be accounted for.

Those of us who are alive have work to do — we have love-making and flower watching. And there's watching the golden eagle. There he is! (She points outside past the sliding glass doors. Soaring and swooping against the backdrop of mountains is an eagle.) They (the Holocaust victims) didn't use up their joy.

In The Far Side of Victory, *you write of the main character Arnie, "Maybe he had never cared enough about anything to fear its loss. If this was so, how vulnerable he was, how fragile he was." Arnie grew to care a lot. You seem to have packed your life with people and causes and work to care about. Do you ever feel vulnerable and fragile like Arnie?*

Yes. The bigger the investment, the bigger the loss. You know and I know — kids sometimes die. Husbands croak on you. They even run away with other people's wives. In order not to chance a big loss, some are willing to settle for less.

And you are not?

No. I have played with the thought, but no. Once you decide, that's it. You do it anyway.

Note: Greenberg's latest two novels are Simple Gifts *(1986) and* Age of Consent *(1987).*

John Hathcock: Alternative Goals

John Hathcock's tiny house in the laid-back mountain community of Kittredge, Colorado, has an equally tiny mortgage. John is articulate, bright, and highly motivated, but he owns no suits or ties, and most of the time he wears faded jeans and running shoes. Except for working the evening shift as a custodian at Marshdale Elementary School in Evergreen, his time is his. Or it could be. He gives much of it away.

For nine years John has coached kids' soccer teams in the Evergreen-Kittredge area. He spends his days off at soccer tournaments picking up pointers to bring back to his team; he devotes afternoons to poring over books on soccer to glean some new strategy or play.

"I guess I just like kids in general, and I love the game of soccer," he explains. "I often prefer kids' company to adults. I like their honesty and straightforwardness." A shy, thirty-seven-year-old bachelor, John has a long, carefully trimmed reddish-brown beard and soft brown eyes with laugh lines radiating outward.

We are sitting in the living room of his three-room stone and wood cabin, which is within sight of the Kittredge Post Office. The gentle valley is filled with small houses such as John's, but with the surrounding rugged hills, evergreens, profusion of wild flowers, and clean, crisp air, the atmosphere is peaceful and quiet. Denver seems much farther away than a twenty-mile drive down winding, two-laned Highway 74.

Soccer paraphernalia is all around us. Cigar boxes stacked on an end table hold the soccer patches that John collects. In a small alcove off the living room, soccer balls in a big mesh bag hang from a hook. The notebooks in which he records details of each game rest on the back of the sofa. His blue windbreaker, covered with soccer patches, is draped across a chair.

Currently, both in this room and in his life, soccer dominates, but other interests are evident. A guitar leans against an armchair. A whimsical pottery goblet sits atop a cabinet. A ceramic sunburst, its face spread with an equally pleasant grin, decorates a wall.

John, a largely self-taught artist and potter, designed and created both pieces. He has sold his work, and could sell more, but he is not producing much lately.

I met John in 1977 when he began coaching with the Evergreen Junior Soccer Association, a recreational league for children. My son, Tim, was on that team — the Bears — made up of fifteen coltish six- and seven-year-olds.

At first the team lost game after game, but gradually, after several years of playing together, they evolved into champions who lost only two games in five seasons. In 1982 most of them tried out for a new competitive team, and almost all made it. John became coach of that new team.

Eventually my son quit. Eventually John felt drawn back to coaching younger kids and he started another fledgling recreational team, the Mustangs. At this writing, they have won thirty games, tied four, and lost one.

I learned a lot about John by observing him at games on frosty fall mornings, at games on soggy spring afternoons, at grueling midweek practices. Besides teaching the kids how to win, he was drilling other qualities into them: sportsmanship, fair play, losing with some degree of grace, and getting up after a soccer ball or another kid knocks the wind out of you.

John taught them — most of the time anyway — without jumping up and down, yelling, or putting anybody down. He simply put his arm around players' shoulders and aimed a few softly spoken words their way. They got the idea. I watched kids respond to being treated with fairness and dignity.

Since settling in Kittredge ten years ago, John has had many activities that have revolved around kids. His first job in the area was driving a school bus, and for nine years he transported kids over the mountain roads. During summers, until 1983, he taught at the Childrens Center, a preschool in Evergreen. For several years he held art classes for children in his home on Sunday afternoons, and he also taught children's karate classes. John holds a brown belt in tae kwon do.

Occasionally, someone offers John a job with more money or prestige than the ones he's worked at these past ten years. A few years ago he tried working at a friend's newspaper, selling advertising space. He lasted just one day. On the other hand, John is known as one of the best salesmen in the Evergreen Junior Soccer Association when it comes time to recruit soccer coaches. Apparently, it's all what you believe in.

John believes in kids and he believes in making an honest living. The rat race is not for him, any more than three-piece business suits are. He is not even remotely self-righteous about his choices, and he is basically satisfied. Here is what John thinks about coaching, kids, work, happiness, freedom, and life in general.

Conversations

What in your life gives you the most satisfaction right now?

It's coaching. After we play a really good soccer game, I feel better than at any other time. Especially if something happens that hasn't happened before — say our halfbacks start getting into position to take shots, and finally see how to execute them.

Right after a game I'll come home and go over my little data book and see who scored, and then I'll record other statistics. After this, I start looking forward to the next game. I can't think of anything else that gives me the same enjoyment.

Why are you so committed to coaching kids' soccer?

Coaching is a lifesaver for me. It's one of the few situations where I can really release a lot of energy. It *seems* that I'm giving a lot to the kids, and I am — but I'm getting a lot too.

A physician who coaches in our league once said to me, "I don't know how you get so much out of your kids."

"Well," I answered, "I can spend a lot more time on coaching than you can. You have your own family and a busy practice, and I don't."

I spend a lot of time coaching. I neglect other things. I've been wanting to fix up this place for a long time. I'd like to clean up more out there. I'd like to put up a fence, but with working and soccer, I just don't have the time. But I do find the time to spend a whole day watching a soccer tournament!

Are you a "confirmed" bachelor?

I haven't married because I just never met anybody I felt I could live with for a lifetime. There are times when I feel like I'm not an "official" citizen without a wife and kids. I value my freedom, and I don't have a lot of bills or belongings. But sometimes I feel that it might be too late for me to raise a family if I decided to. If the right person came along, maybe a lady who's divorced and has a kid. . . .

It's strange to look back and ask yourself why you made certain choices. I feel a little like a character called Malachi Constant in Kurt Vonnegut's novel *The Sirens of Titan*. He travels all over the universe. Finally he manages to get back to earth. When people quiz him about his adventures, he just answers, "I was a victim of a series of accidents, as are we all." That's how I often feel.

I'm not sure why I ended up where I am, doing what I'm doing. I only know that since early in my life, I've been restless. I've always been more interested in discovering things firsthand, not by sitting in a classroom.

This restlessness led me to spend a couple of years — 1971 and 1972 — hitchhiking after I got out of the Navy. I come from Amarillo, Texas, from a typical suburban area. Dad wrote advertising copy, and I was used to the comforts of a nice home. So I had a backpack, a sleeping bag, extra shoes, extra everything.

Early along in my hitchhiking I met a guy who traveled with nothing but his clothes. He had been on the road for twenty years, and he was only thirty-three at the time. At first I didn't trust him, but I soon discovered I could. He didn't steal, he didn't even want money. His religion was the road.

If he was walking down the road and it was hot, he would hang his coat on a fencepost and keep going, confident that the road would give him another coat when it got cold again. I could never have lived that way, but I respected his strength and his faith. Compared to him, I felt like a tourist in a Winnebago.

In a way, he probably reinforced my desires not to become tied down. I did settle down here in Kittredge, but I've stayed away from accumulating lots of things.

How did you end up in Kittredge?

While I was hitchhiking, I got to Boulder, Colorado. For six months I worked as a custodian and doing maintenance and cooking. One weekend a friend asked me to come along and camp out in the Kittredge area. I fell in love with the place and just stayed. At first I rented this house. Then when it came up for sale, I was able to buy it.

I needed a job when I first came, so I started driving a school bus. I found out pretty quickly that the actual driving was only one skill I needed. I also needed some knowledge of child psychology. I started studying books on developmental psychology. I took classes.

At first I thought I could control the high school kids by making them think I was real tough. I wore mirrored sunglasses and chewed gum and would just stare at them as they got on the bus. Finally another bus driver, a Vietnam veteran and ex-New York City policeman, set me straight. "The real trick is to make *them* feel tough," he said. His way was to tease the kids, saying, "Please don't mess with me. Don't hit me." And it was like pushing a button. They responded.

I learned, too, that kids want to know what they can and cannot do. They want to know the limits and rules. Mine were — you can't stand up on the bus. You can't throw things. You can't take other people's belongings.

But even though they want rules, they'll test you. They'll take a little piece of paper, for instance, and throw it. When I'd see this, I'd say to the kid, "You threw something." The kid might answer back, "Well, that little wad of paper was too small to hurt anybody." Then I'd say, "The rule is not against throwing things that hurt people. It is not against throwing big things or little things. The rule is against *throwing*." I did this matter-of-factly. We didn't argue. My stance was simply that they had made a mistake, and that I was there to remind them of the rules.

Do you use psychology in your coaching too?

Absolutely. The soccer field is a great place to teach kids. If a kid has been knocked down and he's angry, and he wants to get back at the kid who knocked him down, you can grab your player right then and there and talk about sportsmanship and control. When the actual situation is occurring, you have a perfect learning situation, unlike just talking about it all day.

The kids listen to you. Do you listen to them?

I'm not only willing to listen to them, I'm anxious to hear what they're saying. If I'm talking to an adult and a kid has something to say, I'll interrupt that conversation to listen to the kid. I feel that what kids are saying is important.

There are times when I won't listen though. If a kid has gotten a minor injury in a game, for example, and is trying to get extra mileage out of it, trying to gain special attention, I'll ignore him.

You enjoy the kids and soccer so much — how about your work at Marshdale School?

I can't say that I "enjoy" it. But I like what I'm doing, and I'm happy just with being free. Right now if I wanted to, I could drop everything — just leave — sell my house, quit my job, go somewhere else. If I was a bank president it would be a lot more difficult.

I should say, though, that I occasionally wonder what that would be like. Sometimes you hear of an executive who chucks it all to work as a custodian — well, at least he knows what he's left behind. I can only guess. And becaue I never finished college, I did limit my options.

Also, I'm working on myself not to be embarrassed about being a janitor. Sometimes another coach will ask me, "What do you do?" Sometimes I just answer, "Well, I work over at the school."

I hate myself when I say that, because I'm just letting that person assume that I teach. This work I do is considered a lowly profession in our society. Whether I choose to be a lowly person because I occupy that profession — that's my decision. Sometimes it's a struggle to keep a feeling of dignity while I'm vacuuming the floors and dumping the trash. Yet that gives me the time to do the other things I really enjoy doing. I don't think a high-powered job that took up all my time and even gave me more money would give me the same satisfaction I get out of coaching and having a relationship with all these kids.

Someday I might switch back to bus driving. That job had a lot of rewards. I drove a bus for handicapped kids who were attending special classes. One little girl was severely retarded and I felt sorry for her. She was so cute, but I knew she was going to grow and her mind was not.

We were talking one day while my bus was waiting for a transfer bus. We always used to play word games when we had a few minutes. I was asking the kids, "What would you like to be when you grow up? If you could be anything you wanted, what or who would you choose?" She answered, "Johnny." A whole flood of emotion came over me. I didn't know how to deal with it, so I just changed the subject.

I like it when I influence the kids in some good way. After all these years in one spot — first driving the bus and working at a preschool, then coaching, I know a lot of parents and kids. Now some of the kids aren't kids anymore.

Not long ago a girl who used to ride my bus filled my prescription at Evergreen Drug Store. She remembered me. I feel special to be known by so many people. I like being part of their lives.

Do you have a philosophy of life per se?

Mine ends up being a pretty simple philosophy. I just try to get along with people, and I try not to do things that would be harmful.

I might go back to school someday. I might even get a degree so I can teach. But right now, I have all I want.

Chet Hover: Blooming Where You Are Planted

Ostensibly because her house is no longer beige as I remember it, but grey now (but most likely because she knows how easily I get lost), Chet Hover stands outside on her front lawn waiting to flag me down. After so many years I could drive on past her house, which looks much like the other small, ranch-style homes planted up and down the hilly Bear Valley area in southwest Denver.

Almost fifteen years have passed since I moved away from the neighborhood and lost all but an occasional Christmas card connection with Chet. Before that she and I often visited for coffee and conversation, and she babysat for my two sons.

I see her waving out front, and as I pull into her driveway memories rush to the surface: Chet comforting me when my second son was born prematurely and had to be placed in an incubator; Chet, not just babysitting, but taking care of my sons as if they were her own; Chet encouraging and mentoring me when I was a young mother nearly drowning in diapers and chronic fatigue.

We hug each other and I look at my long-time friend. At fifty-six, her hair is still more golden brown than grey. Her large blue eyes, always hopeful, have not been dulled with any detectable cynicism. She wears jogging shoes, grey corduroy slacks, a white blouse, gold loop earrings, and a warm smile.

We go inside where she introduces me to Mollie, her impish six-year-old granddaughter, who says "hi" and then bolts outside to play before afternoon kindergarten begins. Mollie, as well as her older brother and sister, are living with Chet and her husband Noel until the school year is over. The Hover's sixteen-year-old daughter Becka is still at home, too.

I had forgotten how dramatic and articulate Chet is until she begins to tell me about her present life. Her voice has a way of sliding up and down — contralto when she is making a serious point, soprano when she is poking fun or making a mock complaint.

Her accent is almost neutral and is missing the Chicago twang she might have picked up from being raised there. But every so often a dash of aristocratic British pronunciation passed on from a thoroughly English mother changes words like "neither" to "nither" and "been" to "bean." (Chet was christened a proper English "Chelsia" but goes by her less formal nickname.)

"There have been wall-to-wall people here for years," Chet says. "But you should have been here *last* year." She pauses, then goes on as if relating something from Ripley's Believe It Or Not. "Last year, my mother and Missy (the Hover's eldest daughter, the mother of the three grandchildren) lived here, too. Neither Noel nor I know when things are going to be easy for us. We've been married almost thirty-three years. When do we get to the easy part of our lives?" In the same breath, before I can respond, she adds, "And guess what? I've decided to become a foster parent in just a few weeks."

Chet has always liked taking care of others and doing her part in the community. She was a Campfire Girls leader when Missy was growing up. "Didn't we all do Campfire Girls?" she remembers, laughing. She worked on the KRMA Channel 6 (Denver's public television station) annual fund-raising auction from 1970 to 1985. And now she is on the accountability counsel for the Denver Public Schools, as a representative from her grandchildren's grammar school.

Chet attends Garden Park Church, a small evangelical, Mennonite Brethren congregation. She has been in charge of Beginner Church there, an alternative for restless four-, five-, and six-year-olds who have trouble sitting still during adult services. She has also led women's Bible study groups and taught a variety of Sunday School classes.

Over the years, Chet has worked at part-time secretarial jobs and has cared for children of working mothers in her home, but she has remained primarily a homemaker. That vocation of hers is what our conversation is about. As we talk, there is no martyrish-look-at-what-I've-sacrificed-to-stay-at-home attitude. And she does not pretend to be a perfect homemaker either. "I don't bake cookies, and I am certainly not much of a housekeeper," she says.

But Chet excels at something which is often elusive and uncommon today. She has an ability to nurture others — to listen, counsel, and really "be" there when she is needed. By "blooming where she is planted," she has made a significant impact on three generations of family and a wide circle of friends and acquaintances.

We sit in comfortable high-backed chairs in her living room. A grandfather clock ticks in one corner. An old pump organ is spread with sheet music. On an early American wing-backed sofa rests Mollie's Raggedy Ann doll. The doll's arms are spread wide open, like Chet's have been for over three decades.

Conversations

Let's begin with your family — what's everyone doing now?

Noel is still part owner of a hearing aid company, Maico of Colorado, in downtown Denver, and he runs the service department. Noel II is thirty. I told him, *no more birthdays!* He's a paramedic at Denver General Hospital, and he's getting a masters degree in computer science. His wife, Donna, works for a mortgage bank that makes home loans. She was just put in charge of a neat new program, which doesn't make me very happy, 'cause I think, now they'll never have kids.

Daughter Missy is twenty-eight. She dropped out of high school to get married the first time. Now she has graduated from Red Rocks Community College — the first woman there ever to graduate in fire science. She would like to go into fire prevention, but getting hired by the fire department is not so easy for a woman. She's working at an emergency clinic and she wants to get paramedic training soon.

Missy just got married for the second time. She and the children have lived with us the past three years, since her divorce. When she got married again and moved out, she decided she didn't want the children to change schools, so that's why they are with us until the summer.

Becka is sixteen and a junior in high school. She is a runner, both cross-country and track, plays the cello, is in National Honor Society, and would like to run away to England to marry "Duran Duran," all five of them!

And you're going to become a foster parent, too?

Yes — I've requested a newborn. But first, Noel and I are taking a vacation. Our kids gave us airline tickets for Christmas and we're going to Tucson and Phoenix. Noel's never been on a plane that didn't have a propeller!

Then, when we get back, I'm sure the folks at Denver Social Services will have a baby ready for us. I told them I don't want anything that walks or talks. I have all the walking, talking bodies here that I need! Besides, I *like* infants. I think I'll have a chance to help the babies' young mothers, too. Part of the reason they don't take their babies home is that they don't know how to care for them. I'm hoping I can help show them.

I understand your mother lived with you last year, too.

Yes. She died this past January. She was almost ninety. There were eight of us in this house then — it's not the biggest house in the world. (Counting a partially finished basement, their house has 1,200 square feet.)

How did that year go?

Well, not too bad. All the grandchildren did very well — they would just plunk themselves down in her room and watch television and keep her company. And mother did fine. The adjustment was hardest for those of us in between.

All her food need to be pureed, and I had to bathe her. Also, she was a semi-invalid and experiencing some confusion. But I did not like having her in a nursing home. We tried that for a year. They took good care of her, but really, it was easier having her here than visiting all the time.

Did you major in home economics in college?

No! I majored in history and English. I graduated in 1950 from a part of Tulane called the H. Sophie Newcomb Memorial College for Refined Young White Women. (She laughs heartily.) Times have certainly changed, and for the better, haven't they? When I finished all that high-class education, I went back to Chicago to Katherine Gibbs

Secretarial School so I could learn some skills to earn a living. I hadn't met Noel yet.

Did you ever plan to be anything but a housewife and mother?

Not really. I've got to admit that I never liked working outside the home. I feel in lots of ways that women of my generation had more choices than women have today. Now, a woman graduates from college and if she says she's simply going to get married, people say, "Oh," as if she is really stupid!

In those days, if a woman wanted a career, she pursued one because *she* wanted to. Today's society says, married and at home is what you are if you haven't got the brains to do other things.

When I got out of college, there wasn't this kind of attitude or pressure. Even now if married women my age are asked what they do, they will usually say, "I'm married and I'm a doctor." But now a young woman would never say that — the attitude is, "I'm a doctor, and oh yeah, I'm married." I think marriage is more important than that. A union as close as marriage really can't be all that secondary.

The world today says to women, you can have it all. There's no such thing as "having it all." Something goes. There are only twenty-four hours a day for all of us.

When a working woman comes home at night, she's *responsible!* Men come home and *eat!* There are some with working wives, like my son, who do more than half the cooking. But a lot of this generation of men is still used to a mother at home. So they want their wives to do all the things their mommies did, *plus* bring in revenue. It's tough today for young women.

Do you ever feel you've sacrificed your own personal goals to stay home?

This is what I *wanted* to do.

What has been your biggest satisfaction over the years?

It's that I feel that I have done the best for my kids that I could. My best may not be the best in the world, but it's the best I could do.

My child psychology wasn't so great in all cases. I made a lot of wrong choices along the way. I said things I shouldn't have said. I did things I shouldn't have done. But at least I was here for them, and I've been here for my husband.

I feel the same about having the grandchildren here. They know when they come home that somebody's going to be here who loves them, who wants to see them, and cares about them. To me, that's the only thing you can really give in this life.

So do you feel your life has basically turned out the way you wanted it to? Marriage. Children.

Not exactly . . . I *am* content, but I thought I'd do all this AND write the great American novel!

My mother always used to say, "Do the best you can every day." I knew, back when I was young, my best was really pretty good. And so I thought that if I did my best, I would accomplish something really great!

But as I have discovered — some days my best is merely getting vertical and getting out of bed! If each day you think, I did as well as I could manage today, and not, I *could* have done better — if you look at it that way, you will be content. But if you keep thinking about all the things you *could* have done better, you might as well throw yourself off the roof. We all have low ebbs in our lives.

If I had to put a motto up — for myself or anybody — I think it would be, "bloom where you are planted." I used to say, "Lord, here I am. Send me on some great mission." And I found His answer was, "Great, start with washing your kitchen floor." And I would say, "No, not that! I want to do something really great." And He'd say, "That is really great for you."

If we want to have joy, we have to find it where we are, right *now.* My older daughter has been through some unhappy times. I think she struggles — as we all have — thinking that someone else can make her happy. But if you are not happy with yourself, nobody is going to make your life happy. Even if they seem to, what happens when they are gone? They could be gone in an instant, and then where would you be?

It's better to find peace inside yourself, because all things become boring after awhile. The best job in the world — climbing Mount Everest for the twentieth time. . . .

How can we find contentment within ourselves?

By letting go of the people around us in any sense of demanding that they fill all our needs, I think. We have to come to the point of being able to say, "It's not up to you to entertain me, love me, hold me, fulfill me, support me."

For me there is only one constant. If I keep my eyes on Jesus, he's the only one who is always going to be there. Other people can be just as crummy as I am. When someone hurts me or disappoints me, how am I to say that in the same circumstances I might not have done the same thing and probably have?

Are you looking forward to taking a turn "doing your own thing?"

Where did we ever get the idea that we can take turns? Life's not like that. I *am* doing my own thing right now. I sacrifice some. My husband sacrifices too. We give to our kids and to each other. They give back to us. If this sounds like something I'd like to get out of, believe me, it's not.

Ed Kurz: The Proverbial Sayings of One Lawyer

"I think it was Coco Chanel who said, take life like a toboggan. Don't look back. Look forward. Enjoy the ride."

Without so much as taking a breath, the man seated across from me continues tossing out upbeat sayings. "If you don't try, you'll never succeed. If you fail, at least you know you've tried."

Denver lawyer Ed Kurz sounds like a combination Norman Vincent Peale and living volume of *Bartlett's Familiar Quotations*. Listening to his quotes is like eating peanuts — it's hard to stop with just a few. Still, before plunging into this interview about the proverbs and quotes by which he lives, I *had* planned on asking him some preliminary questions.

"Excuse me," I interrupt. "Could we backtrack just a moment? Could you tell me about yourself?"

Kurz puts aside the maxims he has been sharing so enthusiastically and fills in some of the details of his past. "I was born in Chicago on March 8, 1921, and raised there," he says in a flat, slightly nasal twang. "In September 1940, when I was nineteen, I joined the National Guard in Chicago knowing that in just fifteen days they were scheduled to go on active duty. In December 1942, I graduated from Officer's Candidate School and after that I was on my way to New Guinea and then on to the Philippines. I finished the war as adjutant of a training center near San Marcelino, in the Philippines, just outside Manila," he recalls.

Kurz, who entered the army as a private, was discharged in 1946 as a captain. Like many veterans who had been forced to defer college, he was anxious to pursue his degree. Ten days after his discharge, he enrolled at the University of Denver. "I had never been to Denver, but a friend said that DU had a good accounting school," he explains. By 1948, in just two years, he had completed a degree in accounting.

While working as a certified public accountant in Denver, Kurz returned to the University of Denver in 1951 to enroll in law school. Again he completed his work rapidly, and in 1953 graduated with a J.D. degree.

For over thirty years, Kurz has practiced law in Denver, and for the past six years he has worked part-time as a referee in Denver's Small Claims Court. "Some people say, 'I wouldn't have your job if it were the last job on earth,'" he comments wryly about his job as referee in Room 31 in the dim basement of the Denver City and County Building. "I can appreciate that," he continues, "but somebody has to do it. Besides, I like it." Kurz has been spotlighted in feature stories in the *Rocky Mountain News* and the *Denver Post* and is well-known for his folksy, informative pre-hearing speeches. He has a reputation for being kind, matter-of-fact, and firm as he dispenses justice.

Now in his early sixties, the 6'1", 220-pound man has black hair greying just slightly and brown eyes which seem permanently backlit with enthusiasm. Besides enjoying untangling conflicting evidence in "people's court," — which he smiles and dubs "the court of best recollection," — he also enjoys dancing, bowling, and golf. He attends the Kiwanis Club of South Denver regularly and has held practically every office in the organization, including lieutenant governor of his division of thirteen clubs. He is also an active member of Grace Lutheran Church and was building committee chairman when the present church was built in the 1950s.

Ed and his wife, Lavonne, whom he married thirty-two years ago, have raised three children. "I feel that having a happy family life all these years is my greatest achievement," he reflects. "We have tried to instill in our children a positive attitude. I think they will be able to do whatever they want to do."

All three are off to a good start; all are graduates of Colorado State University. Sharon has a degree in business administration, works at Hewlett Packard in Greeley, and is married. Kevin has a degree in construction management and is a construction superintendent for Summit Constructors, Inc. in Denver. David, a civil engineer, is attending Stanford on a scholarship, pursing a graduate degree in civil engineering.

Kurz has been through the inevitable low points in life. Besides making it through the Depression and the Second World War, he has also survived personal setbacks. In 1962 he ran for the state legislature as a representative from Denver and lost by only 1,200 votes. More recently, a small business in which he was involved did not pan out. And, after half a dozen years on the bench in small claims court, he has not been appointed a district or county judge — a position he would like.

"I have a good judicial temperament and the ability to listen. The current trend, though, is to appoint younger persons," he says with obvious disappointment.

Still, Ed Kurz is an optimist. For years he has been collecting inspirational quotes — someone else's or his own originals. Some are carefully arranged under the glass on his desk top in his law office. Others he frames and hangs on the walls. When we talk, he has assembled those quotes he wants to share. They are arranged in several neat stacks on the dining room table of his Denver home.

As Kurz shuffles through them, light from the chandelier above reflects off his wedding ring, which has the soft patina of gold worn for a long time. On his right hand, his heavy gold and green high school class ring flashes. Photographs of his children hang on the surrounding walls.

Much of the evidence on Kurz' life is in. He has managed to practice what he preaches. For that reason, the homespun lawyer-philosopher is a person worth listening to.

Conversations

Where did your love for maxims come from?

(He hesitates.) I've been on my own a long time. My mother died when I was three, and my father was away from home quite a bit. I went to work at a young age, and I worked at a lot of different jobs. Maybe because I had to make my own way, I started to make up my own philosophy early. And these sayings just reflect what I came to believe.

For instance, I learned early that you make your own circumstances.

You can't go around blaming people for what happens to you, and you can't look back. All you can do is learn from your experiences.

What is your basic philosophy of life?

I try to follow the golden rule. "Do unto others as you would have them do unto you." (Luke 6:31)

I treat the plaintiffs and defendants in small claims court the way I'd like to be treated if I was where they are. In small claims court you cannot bring in an attorney as an advocate. You have to plead your own case.

This means, as a referee, I have to guide people. I have to tell them what the rules are. I have to be careful not to cut them off before they've had their day in court. I know they're nervous, so I try to put them at ease.

When I first went on the bench I was probably more "pro-landlord" than I was "pro-tenant." But now I'm becoming more deliberate in my findings in landlord-tenant disputes. I'm finding too often that landlords are not playing fair with tenants. It's only because of the advent of small claims courts that tenants are finally getting their due.

Sometimes I have to twist arms in court. I don't try to break them, however. And that goes back to the golden rule. If everyone followed it, small claims court would not be so full. But when something happens, people tend to look around for somebody to blame, or to sue.

"On any given day, anything can happen." This is one of my favorites, and I see this constantly in court. But it holds true for life in general, and I tried to instill this thought in my kids as they were growing up.

When my son, Kevin, was eight, he was going to race a young man from down the street at field day at school. Kevin kept saying, "I can't beat him." And I kept telling him, "On any given day, anything can happen." I was the judge that day. I was scared, and I just kept hoping that the race wouldn't be very close. Because if it was close, to avoid appearing biased, I would feel compelled to name the other child the winner, even if I thought my son actually won. Believe it or not, the other young man slipped in the gravel at the start. My son won by a good two or three feet. The other boy *was* a better runner than my son. But on that particular day, he slipped.

Another phrase I used a lot with the children is this: "Is the moment of pleasure worth the agony which may follow?" I always told them, I don't care what you're doing, telling somebody off, passing a car on a curve, anything. You've just got to be careful of the consequences.

I try to follow this myself. Two weeks ago I wrote an angry letter. I felt better after I wrote it, but I didn't mail it. The other day I revised it, saying what I wanted to, but toning down the anger. Then I mailed it. I decided I wouldn't gain anything by sending the first letter out, except possibly to incur the wrath of the other party. Maybe sending it would have given me some pleasure, but would it have been worth it?

Do you know the serenity prayer? "God grant me the serenity to accept the things I cannot change; courage to change the things I can; and wisdom to know the difference" (Reinhold Niebuhr). Well, Robert Schuller has come up with a new one. "Lord, give me the guidance to know when to hold on and when to let go, and the grace to make the right decision with dignity." Schuller's prayer really hit me. I was involved in a business which wasn't going well. My partner and I — two different kinds of people — had clashed. I was feeling a lot of stress, and then one Sunday morning I heard Schuller share that prayer on "Hour of Power." After this I went to my partner and said, "Buy me out." I lost money, but it was worth it not to keep on trying something which was just not going to work.

In their sixties, people think about retiring, or slowing down. You're not following that pattern. Why?

Well (he smiles and picks up another index card), I feel that "service is the rent we pay for our space on earth."

My work, my profession, is part of my obligation, but I believe that many things must be done on a volunteer basis. I've been active in the South Denver Kiwanis Club since 1962. We've painted houses for people, we've paid for kids to go to camp at Beaver Ranch near Conifer, we've constructed buildings up there. It's better when people volunteer to help others, or when an organization like Kiwanis volunteers, rather than having government always do these things.

And in addition to concrete things, there are other ways of paying the rent we owe for being on this planet. Ralph Waldo Emerson said, "The only gift is a portion of thyself."

There are gifts of the heart, like tolerance, forgiveness, love, kindness, understanding, and sympathy. You'll never know how much good you can do until you focus on giving. There is no limit if you don't care who gets the credit.

While I passed on a lot of sayings to my children, my younger son, David, made up one that he abbreviates with the letters "TGIF." That means "Toe goes in first." Of course, the foot always follows.

When I'm in small claims court, I'm going to let the plaintiffs and the defendants talk as long as they want, because the longer they talk, the more I'm going to find out about the case, and the better I'll be able to make a decision.

Recently, a woman who in my mind had already won her case put her daughter on the stand to testify. And the daughter's testimony completely changed my mind. It was just a little thing — a conflict with the testimony her mother gave, but that day the daughter put her toe in first, and they lost the case.

Do you believe a positive attitude always means success?

No. Many times, even a positive attitude is not enough to get you to a certain place, a specific goal. Many times you're going to think positively, yet be unsuccessful. But the only people who are successful in everything they do are the ones who never do anything.

You've just got to do the best job you can. If you do what you think is right — even with others telling you you're wrong — you won't stop. If you find out you *are* wrong, as sometimes you will be, at least you're living your life and learning something.

Is your Christian faith central in all you've shared?

Yes. For all my quotes, I seldom quote the Bible. But I always try to remember what Philippians 4:13 in the New Testament says — "I can do all things through Christ who strengthens me." I really believe that.

Besides the golden rule, and that quote from Philippians, I have to add just one more from the Bible. "What shall it profit a man if he gains the whole world but loses his own soul?" (Luke 9:25).

I've always tried to keep that question in mind. My advice, and what I try to live by — "Do what you're doing the best you can. Think about your life in terms of service to others. And life will be good to you." But above all, you must feel good about yourself.

Dottie Lamm: Life After Serious Illness

How do I explain my new centeredness?
A love encompassing even jobs I hate?
It's that all living seems joyous
When the alternative could have been my fate.

— From "It's I!" excerpted from *Second Banana* by Dottie Lamm

In August 1981, when Colorado's former First Lady, Dottie Lamm, entered Rose Medical Center in Denver to undergo a modified radical mastectomy, she could have issued "no comment" statements to the press. She might even have hidden her illness from all but family and close friends. Like former First Lady Betty Ford, however, Dottie chose to talk openly about her fight with cancer. In media interviews, and in the columns she writes for the *Denver Post,* Dottie shared her pain, her fears, and finally, her determined recovery.

In the following conversation, which took place six months after the end of a thirteen-month regimen of chemotherapy, Dottie echoes the feelings expressed in the lines of poetry above and talks at length about the ways in which facing death reordered her life.

When we talk, Dottie still has a skier's ruddy tan, a relaxed expression, and an air of good health. Though not officially free of cancer until five years have passed, Dottie is confident. She has licked her early fears. Her strength is returning, and she is gradually resuming a regular schedule.

Dottie is an attractive and accomplished woman. Now in her mid-forties, she has the lean, athletic figure of a high school cheerleader, which she once was. She is as warm and personable as an airline flight attendant, a career that she pursued before her marriage. She is bright and articulate and holds a masters degree in social work. She worked as a psychiatric social worker at the University of Colorado Health Sciences Center in the late 1960s.

Dottie's commitments have been impressive. She supervised the running of the Colorado executive residence, made frequent speeches, and volunteered her time, focusing especially on children's mental health issues and women's concerns. She also continues to write a column for the *Denver Post.*

For more than twenty years, Dottie has been married to Richard Lamm, Colorado's former governor. The Lamm's two children, Scott and Heather, are bright and healthy. Often they, or some aspect of parenting, are subjects of Dottie's columns.

Even with the many pressures of public life, the Lamms' marriage is still a romantic one. Just after Dottie's operation, her husband wrote a special poem for her, a moving verse about cancer's intrusion into their lives. The poem is included in Dottie's first book, *Second Banana,* published in 1983.

Dottie handles the many parts of her life well. People *admire* that ability, but seem to *love* her for other reasons. Friends sum up her personality by describing her as a "very real person." In her column and in person, she possesses an honest and straightforward manner.

As the late afternoon sun enters through the floor-length windows in the sunroom where we sit, Dottie takes off the navy blazer she wears over a pink shirtwaist dress, drapes the jacket neatly over the arm of the wicker sofa, and our talk begins.

Conversations

How have you changed since your illness?

Much more than before, I let myself take pleasure in very simple things. Like looking at the colors that are coming in with spring. When I go jogging now, if I'm on a beautiful street and I want to just walk, so that I can look at the houses and gardens, I do it. I am much more willing now to be a passive recipient of the beauty around. I no longer make all my recreation such a "go-get-'em" kind of thing.

Still, though, there are things that I've decided to improve, and I've worked harder on these. For instance, this year I just decided that I was going to become a better skier. I've been messing around for twenty years! Dick felt the same way, so we took lessons. And I did learn a lot.

There are these two edges of the same thing. Right now I'm running just to stay in shape. I don't care about going for a marathon. I'm not always trying to achieve something in every activity anymore. But I still like to excel in others. Before I was *always* trying harder, *always* trying to be better.

I am really dwelling on the here and now these days, on not being sick, even though statistically I won't feel free for three and a half more years. I've got to be checked regularly right up to the five-year mark. Even then, they never say you're "cured." They say "stabilized." I feel I'm well. I feel I'll pass my five-year test, but I can't just close this out of my life.

There will be two big decisions I have to make during the next couple of years, which makes me a little angry right now, even though I've known it all along. One is whether or not to continue taking a medication that tends to suppress cancer cells. The doctors don't know for sure if this drug actually gets rid of the cells, or if it only suppresses them. If it only suppresses them, then the cells could be in a more advanced stage when or if they pop up later. Would it be better to go off the drug and catch the cancer earlier? This is one of the unknowns.

The second decision has to do with more surgery. When you have had cancer in one breast, surgeons sometimes propose doing a subcutaneous mastectomy in the other healthy breast. Because statistically, if you have had cancer in one breast, the chance of finding it in the healthy breast increases. And when women do get it in the second breast, my surgeon says that they don't recover "as well," but I think I know what he really means. So, this operation leaves the breast intact, but puts an implant in. You look fine, but you don't have the possibility then for cancerous tissues there.

I'm not as brave or as great as people think. There's a thing about wanting all this to be over when it really can't be completely.

Have you received a lot of advice from friends and well wishers?

Yes. The letters I got in the hospital were really interesting. Some said, "Just take time to smell the flowers. Don't worry. Everybody's going to support you during this time." Others wrote things like, "Well, I had the same kind of experience, and I would advise you to stay as busy as possible. Accomplish all you can."

All the letters were nice — that's one of the more pleasant things about having a serious illness. I was really pampered. Both the approaches people suggested might work. One thing is certain. You only hear from the living. You really don't know what the people did who didn't make it.

My tendency has been to slow down, to pick my activities more carefully. Now I'm more willing to stick to my priorities. And for a political spouse, I have always been fairly good at that. I never got into a situation where people had me running all over doing different things I didn't have any interest in.

Still, in your position, isn't this hard?

Yes, I must prioritize even within my priorities. I'm interested in mental health for children, and I have been involved in the women's movement. It's hard to say "no" to people working in these areas, but sometimes I just don't have time to get involved in the particular way they want. Now, I'm comfortable saying, "I'm really for your cause, and I can do this 'little thing,' but that's all I can do right now."

I'm not quite sure why I got ill, but the stress of doing too much might have been a factor. Back during the years of Dick's first campaign (1973-74), I let myself get strung out. And for the first two years that Dick was in office, my body took a lot of stress. I didn't even realize it when I was trying to keep everything together. Dick was busy. The kids were little. It was a hectic time.

I'm not saying that I could never get back into that kind of stressful existence. With teenagers and aging parents — there are always going to be stressful times. That's part of my reason for picking my priorities carefully, and now as I do an overall schedule for the month, I leave empty spaces.

For instance, today is a busy day. Tomorrow is, too, but on Friday, I have all day to put the final touches on a graduation speech I'm giving. If that becomes a half-day job, that's fine. If it's done in ten minutes, that's fine, too. Then I'll have a free day. If, on the other hand, some crisis comes up, I can handle it. I don't feel at all that I have to fill that day.

I guess in some ways I'm living more conservatively, but in others, I'm having much more fun. I have no trouble spending a whole day just having fun! I always had trouble with that before, even when I was doing it. I'd ask myself, what should I be doing instead?

As I've said, I want to put the illness behind me — the bad parts, that is. But I don't want to lose the good parts, the things I've learned. And so, if I start getting caught up in the old mindset of "I need to do this, and I need to do that," then I'll ask myself, "What do you really need to do?" Because of having had that brush with mortality, I'm really listening to myself and my instincts.

How?

Before, it used to frustrate me that I don't work as fast as my husband. But I've learned that my unconscious has to work on things if they're going to be good. My speech or my article isn't going to be very good if I just sit down and grind it out. And Dick's is! I'm not saying my way is superior. That's just the way I have to work. I'm more comfortable with trusting that gut level now.

Dick was extremely sympathetic and marvelous during the year that I was ill. He would say, "You should take a nap. You shouldn't push yourself." But now I think he thinks that perhaps I'm going too slowly in transitioning back. He's trying to be very nice not to say anything, but the other day we were talking and I said, "Dick, are you feeling the illness is behind me and wondering why I don't get on the stick?"

He laughed and said, "Yeah, that's what I'm trying hard not to say." But *I* knew he was thinking this. And if Dick were the one recovering, he'd be rushing back into things more quickly.

Well, now I trust my own instincts more. I used to be more hesitant. If somebody had more knowledge than I did, I would defer to them. If they had more power than I did, I would defer to them. Sometimes, of course, realilty says you have to — but even when I didn't have to, I did.

Most people look at me as having a lot of energy and being very quick, but even with this approval and even with some outward successes, I have tended to feel inadequate at times. But when I was ill, people started telling me how valuable I was. I was very fortunate to be in a position to get public feedback.

Was it hard being in the limelight at such a difficult time?

The publicity surrounding my illness had its down side, but mostly it was positive. I heard from so many people — people who'd read a column six months before and hadn't bothered to write . . . now they wrote. Were some of them thinking, gosh she might die, I'd better write? Whatever the reason was, it made me feel really valued.

Has your illness affected your career goals at all?

Before the illness I saw myself as developing career-wise, just taking off, writing all the time, increasing my work in television. Well, I'm still exploring that but now I'm doing it very slowly, very carefully.

For one thing, I hesitate to become totally career oriented. People have talked about how women are afraid of success, and it's always been put in such a negative way. But I think women who have taken the responsibility for house and children — as much as they may not like some of the things that entails — such women understand that getting into a totally different mindset might remove them from that caretaking role. And they just don't know if they want out of it completely. Maybe some of it is not wanting to relinquish that power at home. With me, I think it's not wanting to relinquish contact with the kids.

Maybe this isn't that clear — here's an example. One weekend I was working on arranging my columns to get them to the publisher. I got so engrossed in meeting that deadline that I literally didn't know where the kids were for a couple of days. That was okay — my kids are old enough and the staff kept track of them. But the fact is, that's not the kind of mother I want to be. I may not want to be *with* them all the time, but I want to know where they are.

When women ask themselves, do I really want to make the tradeoffs it takes to be famous, to make a lot of money, or to "whatever," that's healthy. A lot of men have regretted that they haven't asked the same question. Their kids have grown up, and they never saw them. And the fathers are thinking, where did that time go? Well, nobody stopped them from being with their own children, except themselves. And so, part of my slowing down is because I want to be available. I want to be around.

There is a price tag whichever way you go. Sometimes you just have to pay those prices. I'm not saying you can't have it all — marriage, children, career. Unless you have some devastating things happen to you, and I mean much more devastating than breast cancer, you can have it all within a lifetime. But I don't think you can have it all at once. At least I know that I can't.

Part of the reason I can't is the way my mind works. I tend to really focus mentally, and then I almost use the other things around me as entertainment. I don't want to become so invested in career that the kids and family are like entertainment. Sometimes men do that when they come home. They sip their martinis, then march the kids out to talk a few minutes before bedtime. I don't say all men do that, but that's one pattern.

But you like combining parenting and your careers? Is making your own money part of this satisfaction?

Yes. I have completed a column on the subject of "Wives and Money." I have a hangup. I'm not sure that I should have it. If I really believed what I say, I would agree that there's too much emphasis on monetary value in our society. I believe that homemakers and dedicated volunteers contribute just as much as the people who are earning. Possibly they gain as much or more personally, too.

Still, though, I like to be contributing financially to myself and to the family. My paid work is my writing and television work. I like to be paid for that, and part of this has to do with the dynamics of the family. I want to be earning something. "Something" doesn't have to be all that much, but I need that pay for my self-image within the family. I think, for instance, that it sets a good example for daughters who will be expected to earn. Ninety percent of women will be working within the next thirty years.

Were you tempted, after your illness, to put your careers "on hold," and to focus exclusively on your family?

Actually, I did get back into doing more for my kids when I was sick. I was around more, and I began to realize how much I enjoyed just being around. When my kids' friends came over, I was able to sit down and talk to them. I was not always rushing, not always in the study writing. But now Scott sometimes tells me, "You ought to be out more. You're always on my back."

My children certainly are not babies anymore, but the fact is, they're at ages that I really enjoy. I'm a better mother than I was when they were little. So why should I always be "out there," breaking my neck, and not enjoying them — not that they're enjoyable every minute!

I know it would not work for me or for my kids if I had no other involvements. Since I've been married, I've had to have something that was really my own creativity, my own identity, my own production. You could interchange those three words, depending on what I was doing at different times. I have always had to have something important, but not something all-consuming.

How does this slowing down, this change of pace you've mentioned, fit into your feminist philosophy?

Well, it may not always square with the way others live out their feminism. But I've gotten more comfortable with not having to meet feminist standards any more than I might have to meet more traditional standards.

In terms of issue-oriented things, I agree with practically everything the feminist movement says. But feminists don't have any more right to tell me how to run my life than does the Moral Majority. If a person gets caught up in feminism as a religion or as a "do" or "don't" list of rules, that person is not out of the old trap. She is still boxed in. To me, the ideal of feminism, for both women and men, is the whole business of human freedom and human choices.

But it really is hard on people to have too many choices. I think that this is what Betty Friedan is saying in her book, *The Second Stage*. Ellen Goodman, the columnist, says, too, that women must not go from the feminine mystique to the feminist mistake.

Have you focused more now on the spiritual side of your life?

Yes. Before I knew I was ill, I had felt that I was neglecting the spiritual center of myself and I took a course in spirituality, a week's course at Iliff Seminary (a United Methodist theological seminary in Denver). It was as if I was preparing myself for something, and then when I got sick, I drew on the things I learned in that course.

One of the things people ask themselves after an experience like this is, "Why me?" Rabbi Kushner's bestselling book, *When Bad Things Happen to Good People,* helped me more than anything else I read. Rabbi Kushner says that if you lead a good life, you feel you should be rewarded, not punished. Therefore, when something bad happens, you think, it must have been something you did.

People would rather feel guilty and bad than to feel life doesn't have meaning, that the pieces don't fit together. Rabbi Kushner is saying that certain things are just random. That scares people, because it means that good behavior gives you no guarantees. It means that sometimes life is not fair.

While I'm not sure what caused my cancer, I do think my psychology, my outlook on life, was a strong factor in my getting well. I decided I was going to use my energy and insight to head that direction.

This may sound strange, but I feel more justified in putting myself first now. I realize that if I'm not feeling centered, if I'm not feeling secure and healthy, then the work that I do is not going to be as good — whether it's being a mother, writing a column, or completing a volunteer project.

Since my illness, as more time passes I have noticed that with wellness, I am more likely to get caught up with the "sickness" of letting everyday hassles get me down. I now have to make a more conscious effort to step back from that kind of thing, and get "recentered." Isn't is strange that somehow mental health comes harder, not easier, when one is physically well?

Don Laws: Being the Best You Can Be

When I first met Don Laws, it was several months before the 1984 Winter Olympics. He sat hunched over a plate of greasy hash browns and a Styrofoam cup of coffee in the snack bar of Denver's Colorado Ice Arena. A figure-skating coach, Laws would accompany his protege Scott Hamilton to the games in Sarajevo, Yugoslavia, in February. Then in March the two would be off to Ottawa, Canada, where Hamilton would defend his World Championship title.

That day, over his midmorning snack, Laws mused about taking an extended vacation after those competitions. He talked, too, about slowing down — "giving fewer lessons, working shorter hours" — before returning to the ice to work with Hamilton.

Hamilton won the gold medal, then captured an unprecedented fourth consecutive Champion of the World title. Sarajevo and Ottawa left no more arenas for Hamilton. He had won every competition available to an amateur world-class figure skater. At that point, his coach did seem to deserve the break he had daydreamed about earlier.

Eight months after the winter games, Don Laws and I meet again at the Colorado Ice Arena. Hamilton has now turned professional and is touring the country with a major ice show. Laws, head of the teaching staff at the arena, has just finished giving a young skater a lesson.

"You won't believe this," he say smiling. "I'm busier than ever. The students come, and I can't refuse them. I did get away for awhile. I chartered a trawler and cruised around Chesapeake Bay for several weeks," he adds, sounding almost apologetic that his itinerary was not more extensive.

Laws leads me to his office down a long, cold hallway with a tile floor scratched and gouged by years of skaters clumping to and from the ice. Inside his office it is warmer, and he sheds skates and a bulky pullover sweater, switches on classical music, and sits down behind his desk.

Laws, who is tall and slender with serene brown eyes, silver hair, and a carefully trimmed mustache, is striking enough to be on the cover of *Gentlemen's Quarterly.* He has been on or near the ice for most of his life.

Laws first began skating at the Chevy Chase Ice Palace in Washington, D. C. when he was thirteen. Competition and medals were not on his mind then. "Skating was just an activity that I enjoyed after school and on weekends," he says.

The boy who was skating just for fun soon found himself singled out for a Washington Figure Skating Club Scholarship, which provided free lessons for a year. After that Laws did compete for eight years and in 1950 became U.S. Junior Champion. In 1951 he gained a spot on the world team, placing seventh in the world division competition.

Service in the army interrupted his training, but Laws tried out for the 1952 Oslo Winter Olympics anyway. "I missed the team by one place," he recalls. "Skating and being in the service just did not mix," he adds philosophically.

After his discharge, Laws taught skating in Canada. In 1959 he moved to the Philadelphia Skating Club and Humane Society, the oldest skating club in the United States, where he taught for twenty-one years. It was there, in 1979, that Scott Hamilton began training with Laws. When Laws moved to the Colorado Ice Arena in 1980, Hamilton came to Denver to continue with his coach.

Scott Hamilton's opinion of his coach is clear: "I'd be nowhere without Don Laws," he says. "He not only has a very, very good technical understanding of the sport, he has a way of analyzing why skaters are as good as they are and exactly what they need emotionally in order to improve. He's more than just an 'on the ice' teacher," he concludes.

In addition to his famous protege, the kids around the arena also praise Laws. Young skaters have nicknamed him "the magic man" and parents are eager for him to teach their aspiring sons and daughters. Laws' coaching and teaching produce skaters who are not just accomplished athletically and artistically, but who are also prepared to handle the pressures and prestige of competing — and even the inevitable times of defeat.

Here Laws talks about his career, about Hamilton, and about some of the qualities he thinks skaters (or those trying to gain competence in any field) need. More skating lessons await Laws after we finish. He peels a banana to snack on while we talk, knowing he will not sit down again for hours, and we begin.

Conversations

What did you feel when Scott won the gold medal?

All I could do was reflect. All my energy had gone into the preliminaries, and so I was not that *emotional*, unless you might call the fulfillment of a destiny an emotion. Ever since Scott made the Olympic team in 1980, and I watched him carrying the American flag in the games, I knew that he was destined to become a really great skater. Realizing his gift, I saw my job as a coach and did it. I was just a piece in the puzzle . . .

What did you see in Scott that was special when you first began coaching him?

Well — his physical package. His agility. He looked (he hesitates) — it's hard to find a word! All I can think of is "creature." (He laughs.) In Scott there is a *creature* just made for skating. All he needed was development and a certain amount of direction.

What kind of direction?

He needed to understand that a person can do many things in moderation, but nothing to excess, not even training. Age twenty (when Hamilton began working with Laws) to twenty-five (when he won the gold medal) was a crucial time. He had to learn that you can please some, but not everybody. As he became better known, people asked him for favors and he was invited to lots of places. The world opened up to him and he had to learn to pick his priorities.

I wanted Scott to know that anything in excess is wrong. It's like the word "too." "Too" denotes an erroneous position. Lopsidedness. Something *too* sour indicates an extreme. Something *too* sweet is disproportionate. A correction has to be made when a person is "too" anything.

Did Scott ever lose his perspective?

We all do, and he was inclined at times to become too intent on his skating. When he did, I would say, "It's only figure skating. The door's not locked. You can go out as well as come in." It was not that I wanted him to quit. I just wanted him to be sure he didn't lose his sense of proportion.

When you first began, did you ever imagine coaching someone like Scott?

Absolutely not. I only began teaching skating because I liked skating. It's not that I didn't have the ambition to reach this point, but in the first ten or fifteen years I knew full well there was no way I was ready to teach skaters of Scott's caliber. I was a novice. I hadn't learned anything yet . . .

How did you get from novice to where you are now?

Besides the years of experience, I think that what put me here is surrender. Instead of focusing my energy on what *I* want to be seen as, I have tried to give skaters the skills *they* need to reach their maximum potentials. It may sound like a small point, but if it had been my ambition to train a world-class athlete — if *that* had been my goal, I would have been placing too much importance on ambition and not enough on skaters.

I do care, of course, about my reputation. If I had given this profession less, then I would be seen as less, and I'd be very unhappy. I don't want to be seen as less than I am, or to *be* less.

I think it was Lao Tzu (who is believed to have written the *Tao Te Ching*, one of the basic books of the Chinese philosophy called Taoism) who said that you're never proven a master teacher until those you have taught have surpassed you. In skating, there's a natural progression. In a sport which is constantly evolving, if you find yourself in a position to make the sport something better, to influence the evolution, then you have a responsibility to do that.

If one of my pupils becomes a skating coach, I hope that person will do the job better than I have. Scott has perfected maneuvers on the ice which were unheard of when I was a young skater. I feel successful just being a part of this.

As Scott has pointed out, you are more than an "on the ice" teacher and coach. What other qualities do you try to instill in skaters?

Of course there are the obvious things — training, good instructions, rest, diet — all the things athletes are lectured on. But a skater, or for that matter, any person wishing to become skilled in a demanding discipline — physical or mental — must cultivate some other qualities.

When I say "skater," you could substitute the word "student" or "seeker" or "skier" or "swimmer" or whatever. Skating is just the framework I have experience in.

One thing a skater needs is to develop inner discipline. I try to instill the motivation to do well *within* my students. I don't raise my voice too often when I'm teaching. I don't scold, demand, or reprimand.

It would be easier just to insist and demand. A skater may perform well for a while this way, but then he is merely parroting the teacher and not developing his or her own judgment.

As a mature adult, I make my own judgments for my own life. I try to lead each student toward that same position. I want each one to learn to reason and to come up with a decision without me. Otherwise he will tend to lean on me and not just on me, but on anyone around.

The exciting thing is, if I succeed in teaching judgment, even fifteen or twenty years later the person will still have that ability, whether or not they continued to skate.

I have a whole drawer full of letters from skaters whom I have taught — going back for over twenty-five years. Most of the people I hear from never became top skaters. When they write, they say that skating was not a waste of time for them, but that it taught them discipline and helped them develop as individuals.

Are there any other qualities that you think a skater should have?

A skater needs to want to *win* rather than to *beat* somebody else. In the best sense, a competitive spirit will push him to be the best, to want to excel. But if a skater is simply out to beat someone, then he is focusing on that person, not on himself.

You do need to assess how good each competitor is, and you do need to plan a strategy for doing better than that person. But when a skater starts to despise another skater, really to hate that person, it's counterproductive to self-development. Focusing on a competitor as a means of survival is not good, at least not as anything more than a short-term psychological crutch.

What else?

A sense of refined indifference.

Explain please!

If you want something really badly, you may become very intense and intent upon reaching your goal. Then you may become very tense and begin to insist upon perfection in yourself. You may then turn inward and begin to think obsessively about this goal. At this point, the flow — the creativity — stops.

When I see a skater doing this, I will explain how insignificant skating is in relationship to life in general. I try and get him or her to the point of being able to say, "I really don't care. What does it matter anyway?" This is refined indifference.

And then, with this attitude, things begin to flow again. It is unhealthy and counterproductive just to want one thing to the point of excluding everything else. A skater needs to be a whole person, otherwise he or she becomes not much more than a monkey dressed in a little suit.

But the problem is, young people don't yet understand cycles and periods, beginnings and endings. In wanting to go from "point A" to "point B" as quickly as possible, they are not allowing for the natural plateaus, the ups and downs one experiences in learning or achieving anything.

How about those who do not reach the top as Scott did? Is all the effort really worth it?

As I mentioned before, most of the skaters I've heard from through the years were not the top skaters. But they learned through their experiences. Each competition gives you a better understanding of yourself and of the sport. You become more philosophical, too, knowing that you will not always reach something even when it seems within your grasp. Other people are after exactly what you are after. The prize belongs only to one. All through life there will be jobs that don't work out, relationships that don't work out.

In one real sense, though, there is no losing. You just don't win. You can come away from every competition with something positive, some gain at every level you attain. If you come in fourth or eighth, you haven't lost. You have simply *gained* that place.

It's sad to see youngsters or adults who feel that not winning is a defeat, a loss. Just being out there competing is a very positive thing. It means you're healthy. You're physically fit. You're wanting to do the best you can. And that's all any of us can expect of ourselves.

Note: Don Laws now directs his own skating school which operates out of South Suburban Ice Arena in Littleton, Colorado.

Terry Maxwell: Doing A Job Right

"Dear United Airlines:

I arrived at the passenger check-in area at Stapleton International Airport in Denver less than 10 minutes before the departure time of our flight to Detroit last week. There we were. My wife and I — four children, eight large pieces of luggage and a rental car to return. I excitedly presented my dilemma to Mr. Terry Maxwell and he immediately grasped the situation, decided what had to be done, did it, and more. . . . We were greatly impressed by Mr. Maxwell's friendly, courteous, and efficient service, and even more impressed by the initiative and responsibility he employed. . . ."

When United Airlines skycap, Terry Maxwell, first began receiving "orchid" letters like this one from an attorney in Ypsilanti, Michigan, he saved them in a scrapbook. As time went on, though, he started storing them in large manila envelopes. Today, after over thirty years on the job, he simply reads each one and adds it to the tall stack which fills the bottom of a linen closet.

"I was hired in 1953 as a ramp serviceman — I was the first black man who ever filled that position," Maxwell says. "But soon after, I switched to working as a skycap. That's when people started writing to express their appreciation. And I appreciate every letter, but I've stopped counting them now."

Maxwell is sitting in the living room of his home near Denver's Stapleton International Airport. He has just finished an eight-and-a-half-hour shift and has changed out of uniform into a comfortable blue sport shirt, dark blue slacks, and soft leather loafers.

At fifty-four, he is a striking man with a full mustache and salt-and-pepper hair worn in a short Afro. He is six feet tall with forty-inch shoulders and a twenty-nine-inch waist that he has kept "without even dieting." He has a debonair charm and a soft melodious voice like singer Harry Belafonte.

I asked Maxwell to share some of the letters he has received and he has taken them from the closet and piled them on an arm chair. He leafs through them, glancing at one and then another. Finally, he picks two favorites. "This one's from a nun in New Zealand," he says, breaking into a wide smile.

"It's the first time I've ever had my hand kissed," she writes. "You will be in my book of memories and prayers when I recall my trip to Denver."

"I love this one, too," he says, handing me another from an Oregon nun who says of him, "Your brain is saturated with intelligence. Remove the tinge of profanity, insert the beautiful word of God into you, and you will nearly be the greatest!" Maxwell, a Roman Catholic, laughs heartily at this description of himself.

Before our conversation, I had read a number of other letters and notes from some of the travelers Maxwell has helped — from older people, from the handicapped, from a sprinkling of celebrities including Leonard Bernstein and Marcel Marceau.

It is hard to capture the particular package of actions and attitudes that make Maxwell so outstanding at what he does. A man of deep faith, at work he is a study in light-hearted teasing and boisterous banter. Years ago, one of his supervisors coined the term "The Maxwell Manner" to describe the way he operates.

When I ask Maxwell what that manner is, he answers, "I don't know. I just take care of people. My job is to check you in for your flight and assist you in any way I can."

That Maxwell does, and more. He has also had a second, no less important job, that of raising three children alone.

The children grew up in this neat, comfortable bungalow surrounded by and exposed to the books of philosophy and poetry that Maxwell loves — *The Will to Power* by Fredrich Nietzsche and *The Prophet* by Kahlil Gibran. Maxwell shows me a new book, *Sonnets from the Portuguese* by Elizabeth Barrett Browning, a recent gift from his oldest daughter, Zsa Zsa Rommel. She is a graduate of United States International University in San Diego and works as a social worker in Los Angeles.

His second daughter, Cydney Kim, moved to Kansas City recently to look for work. His only son, Jory Rhett, is serving four years in prison for driving the get-away car in an armed robbery at a McDonald's restaurant in Denver in 1982.

"We talk on the phone a lot," Maxwell says. "He's thinking about taking some business courses when he's released. He's writing poetry now to express his feelings — there's a lot of soul searching in what he writes."

Maxwell, the man who is always helping others and cheering them up, has a sadness in his eyes as he talks. It is obvious that his caring for others begins with his children and that he is suffering along with his son.

He is silent for a moment and looks pensive before he continues. "It is and has been a good life," he says.

Conversations

Which passengers seem to have the most trouble at the airport?

Mothers and fathers traveling with little babies. If I see someone with little ones and they're struggling with diaper bags and trying to get to the gate on time, I recognize what's happening 'cause I've been involved with traveling with three kids and taking care of them. I'll help them get to the gate because I know what they're going through.

Also, I recognize when older people are lost. They may be just standing, looking around. The airport is like a city. They may be wondering where the restroom is. They may not know where the restaurants are. They may not know how to find their gate. I direct them there, and if I have time, I'll take them there. Hopefully someone will take the time to show me when I am old.

My mother was a nurse and she liked people. Although she had twelve kids, she always found time for others. She taught us that if you see a blind or crippled person, you go help them. "Don't laugh at them" she would say. "It could be you tomorrow."

So if I see a blind person, I reach out to them. I tell them who I am and just say, "Let me hold your hand or take your arm." I tell them what's ahead — that the doors are going to open, that there's a step coming up. I talk to them as if I know them.

I understand that the airline gave you the Skycap of the Year Award for the entire nation in 1970. What did that honor involve?

The company gave me a thousand dollars! I put that into a mutual fund which I've added to over the years. I almost missed the award ceremony because the kids were small and it was held in Chicago. This was a formal dinner and I was told the kids could not go with me. I said, the hell with it, I won't go. Then the company offered to pay for a babysitter. So I hired a sitter and flew to Chicago, but during the dinner I called the kids three times, and I flew back to Denver after the award was given.

How did you end up raising your children by yourself?

Well, my wife left with a married man — a neighbor of ours — when the children were four, five, and six. They took the kids with them. I was determined to get them back. I liked being around my kids, and I liked coming home to them.

I didn't know where my wife and this man had gone, so I telephoned his place of work and posed as an FBI agent. I got his employer on the line and told him, "This person is wanted for kidnapping three small kids."

His employer told me that he had quit, but that he believed he had moved to Omaha, and he gave me an address there. Well, I got off the phone, got dressed, got four airline passes, and got on a plane to Omaha.

In Omaha I found the address — it was a rundown old apartment house. I was looking at mailboxes in the hallway to see which apartment they were in when a woman came by and asked if she could help me. I told here I was looking for my "sister" and gave her my wife's name. She told me they had moved, and gave me an address about five miles away.

I didn't have much cash, so I walked. On the way I went through a park and there were these three guys sitting there drinking. I asked them if they knew the location of that address. They did. They took me in their pickup within a block of the house. When I found the house, I just stood there a moment. My son came out into the yard and screamed, "My daddy's here!" And he said, "Daddy, I tried to find you. I went looking for our street, but I couldn't find it."

By this time I had walked up on the porch, and my wife had come to the door. My daughters were there beside her. They looked at me and one of them said, "Daddy, let's go."

The boyfriend was not there. I was so angry I'm afraid I could have killed him if he had been. I took the kids and we went back out to the airport. We had to wait all afternoon for a flight to Denver, and I was afraid my wife and her boyfriend would come find us, but they didn't.

When I got home to Denver with the kids, I called the wife of the man my wife had left with. She knew how much I wanted the kids back! She phoned a few people and they phoned a few more, and that night there must have been a hundred neighbors and friends in this house, right here, all here to celebrate. (Later, Maxwell gained legal custody of his children in court. In the late 1960s, when the judge made this decision, the chances of a father gaining custody were almost nonexistent.)

I didn't have any clothes for them. I wasn't sure how I was going to buy them because before she had left, my wife had charged a lot of things, and I was still making payments on those charges. So I went to Sears and explained to the credit manager that I had my kids back and needed clothes for them. He just said, "Go down and pick out what you want. Just bring the sales slips up to me and I'll sign them." So I did. I bought dresses for the girls and pants for Rhett for every day of the week. I knew with work and everything else I couldn't be washing every day.

What was it like caring for them by yourself when they were small?

I had a lot to learn! At first when I put them in the bath, it was awful! They had a lot of hair and it would get all matted up and I couldn't comb it. So I went to a friend's beauty shop to see her wash people's hair. She would just lay their heads back in the sink and let the water run through. It was so simple! I learned then to wash their hair that way.

While I was at work I had a babysitter. I would come home at night, though, start dinner, put the washing in, cut the lawn, make dinner, feed them. Then I'd do other chores. Later, when they got older, I'd help them with their school work.

While they were having dinner, I would start tomorrow's dinner. I had it all mapped out — what they were going to have for breakfast, if they had clean clothes, all those details. The only thing I never learned to do well was to iron the girls' dresses.

When the children came home from school, I did the same thing with them that my mother did with me. I made them read the philosophers and the historians. They read the same books that I read.

(Terry shows me a letter that his son has written to him from prison. He has penciled faint faces on the page, art which echoes that of Kahlil Gibran in his books.)

He learned that type of art from reading Gibran. The kids read Tolstoy's *War and Peace*. At first they didn't like this reading, but they enjoy these great books now just as I enjoy them. It takes time to appreciate these kinds of works.

I wanted them to have a hunger for knowledge. I have this insatiable hunger for knowledge. I *have* to have something to read each day. Something that means something.

I love all the philosophers. All the poets. Back when I was in the service (from 1950 to 1953, Maxwell was stationed at Lowry Air Force Base in Denver), a doctor I worked with nicknamed me "The Nietzsche" since I like to quote him so much.

I love Nietzsche, Tolstoy, Chekhov, Goethe, Hegel, Kierkegaard, Kafka. I wish I knew what they were thinking when they were writing. How many of them locked themselves away like Henry David Thoreau? Did they hole up in a loft like Nietzsche?

I see almost anything in print and I'll pick it up. It's the same with music, especially the classics. But I adore jazz because I grew up in the era of the greats like Thelonius Monk and Charlie Parker. They called it bebop then. There was Dizzy Gillespie, Lester Young, Count Basie, Duke Ellington — a universe of these guys!

The thing I fall in love with most in a person is his mind. I wanted to be a physician. I went to the University of Colorado on the G.I. Bill and took premed courses — biology, chemistry. But I didn't do too well in the regular math courses — working in the air force, my mind had been channeled toward the metric system. Then I just could not find the time to work and raise a family and go back and take the remedial math I needed. . . .

I had to stop short of that ambition. In my job now, though, I take it upon myself to help people in any way that I can, and I feel good about this.

Do people always respond well when you help them?

I've never had an "onion" letter, never. But I have had several verbal complaints over the years. One was from a lady I called "my dear." When I called her this, she shot back, "I'm *not* your dear." I was startled and I just answered, "Of course you're not!" Then I got a little mad and told her I would never pick *her* for my dear.

She had misunderstood. When I try and act polite to women, I'm not flirting. It's just the way I talk. All women are beautiful — old, young, in-between, skinny, fat, tall, short. They're all beautiful and I like to make them feel that way.

One funny thing happened recently at the airport. The women at the ski information counter are not always busy, so when I'm not busy I go by and talk to them. Well, one day they started recording in a book everything I said to them. Every time I talked to one of them, she'd write it down.

Then finally one day they said to me, "Okay, we *know* you." And I said, "What is your knowledge of me?" (He sounds very innocent.) And they just laughed and opened this book and said, "Look. You told *this* to her, to her AND to her! You told us all the *same* thing." (He laughs.)

Is there anything about your job you don't like?

One thing I hate is being called a "porter." That sounds like the railroad station or like a janitor in a big building. They are called porters. We are skycaps. I also hate being called "boy." Generally, it's old people who do this, so I excuse them and let it go.

And it's hard sometimes with the other skycaps. They can get jealous and resentful. One of them went so far as to suggest that I was having the flight attendants write these orchid letters for me and mail them from different cities! And sometimes they ridicule me for keeping out-of-town newspapers. I like to pick up a *New York Times* or a *Chicago Tribune* when I see one discarded. Sometimes I get mad at them and I say, "May you find continued employment in Hades." If I said, "Go to hell," they would know what I meant and yell back at me!

But these are small things. There have been so many beautiful people in my life. I have so many friends. Captains. Flight attendants. Their families.

And I had my kids all those years, available each day after work. I've had women friends, and I have a good friend now, but we don't have plans for marriage. I enjoy my books, music. I love to watch the world news.

Even without the kids, I come home and I'm not bored. In the winter if it's snowed, I shovel my snow and the widow's next door. And there is another old woman down the street and a man across the street about ninety years old. I shovel their snow and take them to the doctor.

One thing I would like to do and can't afford to do is to retire — not necessarily from the company but from the job, the labor. Working outside in the cold . . . I don't enjoy that anymore. But waiting on people I do still enjoy. I have accomplished as much as a working man could accomplish — raising three kids and paying off this house.

I lost my earthly father before I was a teenager. I served in the air force. I lost my wife and raised my children alone. I believe in God — He's helped me through all this. In fact, He lives right here in this house with me. I feed Him toast and oatmeal and milk . . .

(He laughs softly.)

Note: Terry Maxwell died suddenly on January 22, 1986.

Joan Robertson-Mazak: On Becoming More

For sixteen-year-old Terry, from Denver, the diagnosis is catastrophic. The lump on her shoulder is cancer, a cancer that has already swept through much of her young body. For as long as she can remember, she has wanted to go the Roman Catholic shrine at Lourdes, France. Her family says she has always put others before herself, and if she is able to take this pilgrimage, she wants to pray for everyone's happiness and well-being while in this holy place.

Joan Robertson-Mazak, president and founder of Make-A-Wish Foundation of Colorado, and appointed to the national board of Make-A-Wish of America in 1984, does not know exactly why Theresa "Terry" Law has chosen this one particular wish. Whatever her reasons, Joan and the other workers in Make-A-Wish will put in the hours of work necessary to turn Terry's dream into reality.

Make-A-Wish Foundation was born in Phoenix in 1980 in the dreams of a dying boy who wanted to be a policeman. Officers from the Arizona Department of Public Safety granted his wish with a custom-made uniform, helmet, and badge, and even a helicopter ride. That one child's special delight in having his dream come true provided the inspiration for the foundation. Make-A-Wish will consider the wish of any terminally ill child up the age eighteen anywhere in the United States.

Each wish takes a lot of planning. When I arrive at Joan's suburban townhouse south of Denver, she is on the phone ironing out last-minute details revolving around this one. She lets me in, apologizes for running late for our interview, then dashes back to the phone.

When that conversation is over, she immediately dials a second number. "Here's the message to go with the flowers," she instructs the florist on the other end of the line. "Theresa — Have a good trip, we'll be praying for you." Signed — "Make-A-Wish."

Now she offers me coffee and a wide smile, explaining that the terminally ill girl and her family will receive the bouquet and good wishes before they board their flight. "The little details are important," she says emphatically.

Now in her mid-thirties, Joan looks like an executive who might have stepped from the pages of a woman's magazine. She is tall and slender, with a complexion as creamy as homemade peach ice cream. Her fingernails are long and manicured.

Later in the day she is making a presentation about Make-A-Wish before a community group, so she is already dressed in a tailored rosy beige suit with a plaid scarf billowing from the open neck of a silky beige blouse. On the lapel of her jacket is a delicate gold pin, the fragile wishbone which is the Make-A-Wish symbol.

Because Joan is so flawlessly put together (even though "you'll usually find me in jeans"), and because her traditional living room is serene and in perfect order, it is hard to imagine she has had her share of grief. yet she has. "My daughter Jennifer had biliary atresia — that's a liver disease," she begins. "She was almost eight."

Before Jennifer's death, Joan, a single parent, worked as head of beverage service at the Sheraton in Denver's Tech Center. She supervised personnel, sometimes tended bar, and kept irregular hours. But back then when her workday was finished, it was finished. Today as a genie granting wishes, as a mother who has lost a child, as a lecturer for the foundation, as a media spokeswoman appearing on radio and television, Joan's commitment is twenty-four hours a day. Inherent in her fulltime position at Make-A-Wish is constant confrontation with death, and the necessity of reliving daily her daughter's death.

Here Joan talks about her daughter's death, her relationship with her surviving daughter, Melissa, and her involvement with Make-A-Wish. No, it hasn't been easy.

Conversations

I know it's painful, but would you share the experiences which led up to your involvement in Make-A-Wish?

It's okay. I can talk about them. One of the things I remember the most was about three weeks before Jennifer's death. Someone gave her a stuffed KIMN chicken, and she loved it. And then, just by coincidence, someone else called and said, "Do you think she'd like to meet the KIMN chicken?" I said yes.

(Wearing a yellow-feathered costume, the KIMN chicken, mascot for Denver radio station KIMN, appears everywhere from Denver Nugget basketball games to the hospital room of an ailing child. Known just as Jim, the anonymous agent of good will especially loves children.)

The KIMN chicken came to visit on Sunday morning, and he walked all over the area with her. By then she looked really bad — very distorted, very ugly to everybody but her family.

Her younger sister, Melissa, is very pretty. Kids would make fun of Jennifer when they were out playing. But I continued to take her places and I taught her how to cuss. And if people made fun of her, she'd turn around and let them have it, although she was very meek and shy!

The best part of the KIMN chicken's visit was he wouldn't let any of the other kids touch him, only her. He carried her around while all the others watched. I took pictures that day — the last ones I have of her smiling. His visit was something she talked about until the day she died. It was the first time in a long time that she had something totally hers.

How did you prepare for her death when you knew that the time was close?

I didn't really know for sure until around twelve hours before that she was dying. She died at home. That was the way she and I wanted it. We slept with her during those last hours. It was comfortable. When her father (though Joan and Jennifer's father were divorced, he was with his daughter during this time) and I told her to let go and die, she took her last breath.

We kept her home for three hours after that. We bathed her, washed her hair — and that was good. You can't imagine someone dead unless you have seen them dead. And a lot of people haven't. I hadn't. Once I saw rigor mortis set in, and felt her turn cold, it was the best form of detachment I could have ever had.

Had they taken Jennifer away from me when she was warm, I can't imagine making that detachment. We took her to the hospital to be pronounced dead. We tagged her and took her to the morgue. We stayed with her as long as we could, then the attendant took her. By then I was ready to hand her over.

How could you ever do all this?

Number one, I had almost eight years to make decisions. I always knew she was going to die. Her problem was diagnosed early in her life. It wasn't until her sixth year that I was totally sure what to do with her after she died. I ended up cremating her. Up until that sixth year, I wouldn't have thought of cremation for anything. When I finally chose it, I couldn't imagine burying her.

It took a long time to make the decision on whether or not to have an autopsy. I had to decide what I could live with in my mind. And I had been in hospitals so long during her illness that I could picture an autopsy. I didn't want to have to go to sleep at night thinking about them doing that to my daughter.

The way I've done these things is the easiest for me to live with. I have my daughter's ashes in my bedroom in an urn in a chest with all the things she had since she was a baby. Right now I could not — and I doubt that I ever will be able to — scatter her ashes.

How did your daughter's death lead you to found Make-A-Wish in Colorado?

Jennifer was so sick; and the people of Denver knew she had to have a liver transplant, so about $30,000 had been raised for that, but she died before a chance for a transplant came about. And when she died, I began to give the money away. If I saw someone on TV whose house had burned down — I sent them money. If a kid's parents were killed in a car accident, I sent him money. I found out a friend at work had cancer and I gave him a substantial amount to pay his bills. But I still had some money left and the amount remaining in the bank was earning interest.

I went to the employee council at the Sheraton Denver Tech Center (money had been raised for Jennifer's liver transplant in part through the employees at the Denver Sheraton Tech Center) and asked them if they had any ideas about what I could do with this money. We talked about lots of possibilities, but finally we decided we wanted to do something for children.

I had seen a special program on Make-A-Wish, before Jennifer died, and I remembered how happy Jennifer was when the KIMN chicken visited. Suddenly, everything seemed to come together. I suggested starting Make-A-Wish in Colorado, and that's what we did.

Now that I'm doing this — now that I see the looks on these kids' faces when they are given their wishes — it's the same joy as the KIMN chicken gave my daughter. If giving a child his or her last wish gives the family something to remember — someplace to go, someplace to get away from the hospital — it's worth it.

These families who have a dying child like I did — they still have washing, ironing, and jobs. When you have a sink full of dishes and your daughter wants you to rub her back, it's like, "Oh, God, what do I do first?" We're giving these families a chance to do something that may give them release from the pressure, which is immense. We're giving them one last time together, too, and I understand how important that is.

What are some of the wishes you have granted?

Our first wish involved a six-year-old boy with a brain tumor. He had never caught a fish. We arranged to pick him up in a fire truck with the sirens blasting, and to drive him to a helicopter provided by Public Service. They flew him to Dillon, and we put him up at the Ramada Silverthorne. He caught nineteen fish in an hour at Sweetwater Trout Farm. His is a perfect example of a genuinely real wish.

Our second wish didn't work out so well. Although they were not from India, the boy and mother involved practiced Hinduism and the boy wanted to die in India. But the doctor wouldn't give approval for the child to travel, so that wasn't possible. The boy also wanted to meet a movie star. We tried and tried to contact some stars, but their agents wouldn't put us through to them. Finally we got hold of Lee Majors, who said he'd love to see the child. But the boy died before we could arrange it.

That was our only bad one. Another child had leukemia and wanted to go to Disneyland. We sent her. Before she went, she was getting two transfusions a week, and doctors said she had three months to live. It's been six months since she went to Disneyland, and she's no longer getting transfusions. She's even back in school. Her mother considers that trip the miracle they were looking for.

We have emergency wishes and regular wishes. For each wish we try and get as many hotel and airline donations as possible. Up until yesterday, we'd only spent $400 on all the wishes so far. But this trip to Lourdes has to be done quickly and it's costing $6,000. With corporate donations and private donations, we've never been in the position of having to worry about money, but with a few more $6,000 wishes, we could be.

Does all this take most of your time?

Absolutely. If I'm not doing a presentation, I'm doing my duties as worker, because I do all our office work, too — all our calls, our answers, our thank yous. My job just became a paid position. This way, I'm able to devote full time to this work without going out and getting another job. I make exactly enough to pay my expenses. I don't need extra money to put in the bank — I never was a saver anyway!

This job is hard on my other daughter, Melissa. She's seven and a half now. She went through being jealous of my attention to her sister, and then upset that I wasn't kind and loving during my grieving time. Now, I've given all my time again for her sister, as she sees it.

There was something like a karma between the daughter who died and me. It was almost as if we were one. When she took her last breath, I let out some ungodly sound, like the sound in the *Exorcist*. It was like everything had been ripped up through my mouth, my whole body. I'm sure that's the same feeling other parents have when they lose a child.

I don't have that yet with my younger daughter. I always used to think, I'm just like my older daughter. I used to think that was why we were so close.

Now I realize I'm just like my younger daughter. We have the same personality. We have the same temperament. We fight like cats and dogs. I see now why my older daughter and I got along so well — we were opposites. This never dawned on me until finally a friend said to me one day, "Who do you think you're kidding? You and Melissa are just alike. You and Jennifer were opposites."

What are some of the changes you see in your life as a result of doing this work?

Well, sainthood hasn't come yet, and I don't feel it's ever going to. (She laughs.)

I don't picture myself as what people seem to think I am. I don't see myself at all as an overly warm, kind, giving person. Sometimes when I do something that I consider really rotten, I think about how some people are seeing me as some sort of example. It's really hard when somebody says, "You're a wonderful person."

I feel like saying, "Hey, are you talking to me?" I used to steal candy out of the candy store when I was small. I drank beer in high school. Like most women in this country, I wasn't a virgin when I got married. And now — I smoke. I drink. I cuss. I've been married twice.

If I saw all about me written down on the left-hand side of a page, I wouldn't think that person was a very great person. If I looked at the right side of the page and saw listed there what I've done — what I've accomplished — I'd think that person was a pretty good person.

I know that the only way I've crossed over from the left side of the page to the right is because of Jennifer. But I'm still not sure that being over on this "doing" side of the page is where I should be. Being over here is causing me to give up time with my other daughter.

I guess I never really grieved Jennifer's death. I tried to be strong for so long. I'm letting down now, going ahead and feeling the sorrow. Melissa and I are getting some counseling to help us both. I want to be closer to Melissa. I want to go on with living now — enjoying her and the work I have to do at Make-A-Wish.

All kinds of changes are happening inside me. I'm not quite sure why. I'm not quite sure how. I'm still in this transition time of being what I've always been — which I never thought was all that great — and becoming what I'm becoming.

And it's hard for me to understand.

(Note: Recently, Make-A-Wish chapters throughout the United States had granted over five thousand wishes. In Colorado, 180 wishes had been carried out. And Melissa and Joan are doing very well.)

Ann Moore: From Idea to Industry

Back in 1964, Ann Moore and her mother, Lucy Aukerman, designed a soft fabric carrier for Ann's newborn daughter, Mande. Neither mother nor grandmother ever dreamed of selling the carrier, but when people saw Ann with Mande snuggled against her, content and happy in her fabric cocoon, they wanted one "just like that." And so Ann and Lucy started filling a few orders.

Before long there were more requests from friends of those first buyers. A seamstress was hired, and then several more, and soon a busy cottage industry was humming along. Gradually, the small enterprise evolved into a full-fledged company called Snugli Inc.

And today? Snugli has added more products for babies to its line and the company has sales orders topping $6 million. Ann Moore, ex-Peace Corps member and pediatric nurse, never envisioned all this happening.

I have come to the Moore's house in Evergreen, Colorado, to talk with Ann about how she and her husband, Mike, fashioned her original idea into an industry. Their wood-and-glass house with its shake roof is Colorado contemporary, only more modestly sized than most in this mountain community. It is set down in a cluster of tall pines, just off the main highway which winds down to the interstate leading to Denver.

Most of their neighbors make the daily commute to the city, but Ann and Mike have only to walk a quarter of a mile down a dusty driveway to Snugli headquarters, housed in an old cabin and a larger building which was originally a dog kennel.

After bypassing their house and winding up at the Snugli offices, I am ten minutes late. Ann smiles as she greets me at the door, assuring me, "No problem — I have all morning free." Inside, she shows me to a comfortable chair and asks, "How about some tea? The water's hot."

If I had expected a high-powered "Type A" executive dynamo, the woman sitting across from me could not be further from that stereotype.

In her late forties, Ann is tan, fit, and lean. She wears little makeup and her long hair is brown with broad ribbons of grey. With her soft, soothing voice and gentle manner, it is easier to picture her at work as the trained nurse she is than to imagine her as founder and co-owner of this company.

How did this scenario unfold? Ann tells her story at ease in a living room which mingles plants, primitive wood furniture, artifacts from Africa, and old farm implements.

Conversations

Tell me something about your background.

I grew up on a farm in southwestern Ohio. My parents belonged to the Dunkards, who are very similar to the Amish. They're "plain clothes" people — they do not wear worldly, "store-bought" clothes. That (she points to the wall across from us) was my mother's bonnet, and hanging there beside it — that's my dad's hat. (The bonnet is black, as is her dad's wide-brimmed hat.)

The Dunkards are mostly farming people, who are very family oriented — that's their primary focus.

They also have a list of "don'ts." You "don't" do non-sacred music or dancing, for instance. When I was in sixth grade, my parents were excommunicated because they had a radio. They just wanted to listen to the news, weather forecasts, farm reports — that kind of thing.

But I don't want to emphasize the negatives. The most wonderful thing about that whole community is their love and support for the family. I am very grateful to have grown up in that kind of a nurturing atmosphere.

There were sixteen in my high school graduating class of 1952. Most went right from high school into farming and everybody got married very young. I think I was the only one who went on to college.

I went to the University of Cincinnati to study nursing. After I got my degree, I went to New York and taught nursing at Babies Hospital, which is part of Presbyterian Medical Center. I was working in "peds" (the pediatric ward) and as it turned out, one of the doctors there had talked with Sargent Shriver (director of the Peace Corps under Presidents Kennedy and Johnson) about sending a medical team to Africa in 1962. I joined the team.

But before we went, we had to train at Howard University in Washington, D.C. Mike (her future husband) happened to be there for training, too. He had graduated from Yale and was going to Africa to teach with the education team.

I met Mike on the first day and we started dating right away. It was a whirlwind courtship, but we figured out later that our six weeks together during that training was equivalent to three years of a standard college romance! We were out jogging around the track at five in the morning. We had our last class at eleven at night. So we spent a lot of time together.

We gave Mother and Daddy only two weeks to get ready for our wedding, which we wanted to have at home on the farm. The neighbors — everybody — came in to help. People were so excited that Ann Aukerman was *finally* getting marrried. I was, after all, twenty-seven!

At Yale, Mike had been a member of a singing group, the "Whiffenpoofs." They were like brothers, and he was the first one to get married, so the whole bunch — these sophisticated eastern boys — came to the wedding. There is no drinking among the Dunkards. It was quite a different experience for them, but we had a wonderful time. The next day Mike went off to Africa, and I joined him a few weeks later with the medical team.

So there we were in Togo, West Africa. And it was there that I was so impressed with the African sense of mothering — the closeness that they have with their kids. When the babies would come in, their mothers always came, bringing the rest of the kids, too. And the whole family would stay at the hospital.

To have your mother around when you are sick — what that does, it's amazing. The stress level is so much lower when there is that continuum. We're just now catching on to that in this country. It's so interesting that the real human values in child rearing seemed so much more advanced in Africa, and yet we call *them* primitive.

In the marketplace in Togo, there would be lots of babies, but they would not be crying — not like in the grocery stores here. The babies were content. I noticed then that most of the women just took a long piece of fabric and tied the babies onto their backs. The babies were strapped to their mothers by this shawl. And they showed few symptoms of anxiety, none of the thumb sucking and other nervous habits that babies in the western world pick up.

After two years in Togo, when our time was up, we came back to this country to live with Mike's folks in Denver. (Mike is a third-generation Coloradoan.) And our first daughter, Mande, was born just three weeks later, in August 1964.

I had told my mother about the African shawl that the women used. And when she came to help after Mande was born, she encouraged me to try carrying Mande that way. I did. But Mande kept slipping out of the shawl.

Mother and I worked on designing something that we thought might work. Mother always had one of us on her hip while she was stirring the soup. I wanted this closeness. I wanted to have my hands free, too, so Mande could even ride with me on my bicycle. We didn't yet have a car!

We experimented and finally came up with a carrier which had shoulder straps, an inner pouch for positioning the baby, and an outer one for back support. We added a waistband to keep the baby from bouncing around.

When I had Mande with me in the carrier, people would come up and say, "Wow, where can I get one of those?" I had never thought of marketing them. But I wrote my mother, who had gone back home to Ohio, and asked her if she would like to sew a few of the carriers.

And so we sent the first orders out in brown grocery bags. And things just grew. My mother soon had her neighbor ladies around her helping, and a cottage industry was created in Ohio with those Dunkard women making the original handmade Snugli. Because of the cost, we discontinued the handmade Snuglis later. We have a plant in Lakewood (Colorado) now where the carriers are manufactured.

But initially, you never thought of this as a business?

Oh, never! First of all, my mother and I were not businesswomen at all. I'm much more creative than I am systematic. But fortunately, Mike is more left-brained. So when it appeared we had a business, in 1972 he quit his job. He had been head of the Philanthropic Foundation at Great Western United (then a conglomerate), and then he was director of Denver's War on Poverty.

So Mike handles the business aspects of Snugli?

Yes. He heads the company, and I'm on the board of directors. I still work with product design and development, too, and I handle some customer relations things — I especially like correspondence with customers.

I can push our products (which now include a portable baby bed, diaper bags, a lambskin comforter, and a fabric "Quiet Book") because I really believe in parents and kids getting closer. I think that the hope of the world rests in developing a trust and intimacy with our children. When children bond with their parents, then they feel good about themselves. If they *feel* loved, then they can love.

And you feel that the products you've designed help?

Yes. Just last week a physical therapist called and asked if we had any Snugli "seconds" she could take along to India. She will be at Mission of Hope hospital, where they take in babies who are abandoned on the streets. They're near death usually, and they have to be put in an intensive care unit at first.

These little ones are rehabilitated, and some come back to this country for adoption. I'm glad we can contribute to something like this. I grew up in a home where I was loved and nurtured. But these children have no choice.

What do you think babies need from their parents in order to feel loved?

They need at least one parent who will shower them with quality time. Either the father or mother can do this. Ideally it would be best if both could. But one parent has to schedule enough time to focus exclusively on the baby. A baby can sense a parent's tension or nervousness or distraction. And a baby can also sense a relaxed, joyful, playful spirit.

The problem is, if a parent is under terrific job pressure or is exhausted most of the time, then it's almost impossible to cultivate any kind of quality time.

I am not advocating that women stop working. I really do believe in the advances feminism has ushered in. But, I think that men and women, if they choose to be parents, should give parenting a high priority in their lives. Most young parents today want vocational success. It's great if we can become self-actualized, if we can realize our own personal dreams, *and* do a quality job with our children. But it's tough. It's probably one of the biggest challenges most of us face on a daily basis.

I feel I was a good nurse, but if I am looking at the biggest contribution

I can make to humanity, it is giving back to society children who grow up into loving beings. (Ann did not work fulltime while raising her three daughters. Mande and Hopi are both now attending college. Nicole is in high school.)

I know that I followed my mother's example. I can recall only one or two times in my whole childhood when I came home and my mother wasn't there. She was there so I could tell her everything that happened during the day.

Evidence seems to be proving that if close connection with a primary caretaker or a parent is not developed by a child, then it's hard to establish one later. It seems that with all our technology in this country, we should be able to catch up with other "less-developed" countries in terms of human values.

A couple of years ago we were asked to host three members of the communist party who were on an official visit to this country. One was the editor of *Izvestia*, the Russian newspaper. All were men in their sixties and seventies. Our kids were at the dinner table, and we had invited another family over. A *Washington Post* reporter and translator had come along with them. We had a prayer before dinner, and when the prayer was finished, one of the men said something in Russian. The translator told us he had said, "The hope of the world is in the family."

I was just teary-eyed. Here we all were around the table, with the same thread tying us together. Every society has its own kind of goodness. If only we could focus on that rather than on differences. Basically, we all want to be loved, and we want to love. And that could be bigger than all our differences.

Note: In 1986, Gerico Inc., another baby products firm based in Thornton, Colorado, bought Snugli. The Snugli line is still being manufactured in Lakewood, Colorado.

Reynelda Muse: Superwoman: A Cost Assessment

Reynelda Muse comes to the door and says "hello" in a velvet voice so warm and sincere that her greeting seems to hold more content than an entire welcoming speech. Some people know instinctively how to make others feel at ease. Muse is such a woman.

Over the years, millions of television viewers have welcomed the personable newscaster into their homes. From 1968 until 1980, Muse worked for KOA-TV, Channel 4, in Denver, first as a field reporter and then as anchor on the noon news. From 1974 until 1980, she co-anchored the 5 and 10 p.m. prime-time newscasts.

In April 1980, Muse accepted a position with Cable News Network (CNN) in Atlanta as principal weekend news anchor. Her newscasts reached a potential 30 million viewers from Hawaii and Japan to the Virgin Islands. Because her husband and three children were tied to Denver, Muse chose to commute weekly to her CNN job rather than relocate to Atlanta.

"I spent four and a half years commuting," she explains. She has now returned to an anchor position with Channel 4 (now KCNC-TV) in Denver. "Commuting meant leaving Denver just after midnight on Thursday morning and getting to Atlanta around 6 a.m. Early Monday morning, I would catch a plane back to Denver and get home by 7:45 a.m. It was a great experience, but it is wonderful to be in Denver fulltime again."

Others besides Muse seem pleased, too. Clark Secrest, the *Denver Post's* TV and radio columnist, wrote, "Whether Reynelda Muse is the most effective TV anchorperson ever to smile into a Denver TV camera is a subjective judgment; I happen to think she is, and it's . . . nice to have her back."

We talk in the living room of her partially restored — "there is always another project" — 1888 vintage Victorian home on a quiet old street in northeast Denver. Plants lean toward the morning sun in an old-fashioned bay window. Built-in shelves spill with books and records reflecting diverse interests — Kenny Rogers and Haydn, encyclopedias and *The Vegetarian Alternative*.

Over the fireplace, three African women in turbans stare out from an impressionistic oil painting. African masks decorate another wall. The Muses — Reynelda and her husband, Daniel Muse, a Denver attorney — collect art and artifacts which reflect their African heritage. The couple also chose names of North African origin for their three children — daughter Zain, and sons Akil and Malik.

We are seated on a cranberry-colored sofa with a sprinkling of white dog hairs on a cushion. Of little concern to Muse is a touch of stray fur or a light film of dust on the old oak floors. What has concerned her during the thirteen years she has been a mother is how to balance her career, her relationship with Daniel, and her parenting.

The subject of our interview is the cost of being "superwoman." Clearly Muse is not "typical" and she does not attempt to speak for the majority of working mothers. Earning a high salary has meant having enough money to easily afford babysitters and household help. Her high visibility and success have handed her a large measure of personal satisfaction as well.

On this, a morning off, her three children are at school. The house is quiet. Muse is dressed comfortably in a deep pink sweatsuit which compliments her creamy mocha complexion and draws attention to her expressive brown eyes. She pours two cups of steaming coffee, and we begin. As she explores her feelings and ideas about working, parenting, and holding a marriage together, any working mother who has ever felt guilty or exhausted or inadequate will relate to what she says.

Conversations

You seem to have it all. How do you feel about your life at this point?

The surface of my life *looks* smooth. I haven't had a nervous breakdown, and I feel as if I'm functioning very well. But sometimes I worry about whether or not an unknown toll is accruing — a price I won't pay until I'm forty-five or fifty (she is now thirty-eight). I sometimes wonder if I'm deluding myself somehow. Maybe I'm under more stress than I think I am.

Even now, I don't know whether or not a woman can really have it all. My thesis is pretty much that the jury is still out on my generation. We're the first to have such a high percentage of working women. We are still in transition in terms of so many issues. We're still struggling with how to handle a household and work — how much our husbands will or won't do — how we manage to find time to nurture our children.

So you sense there is a price?

Oh yes. For years I used to believe that you could do it all, that there was really no essential cost. But I've had a monumental shift in my awareness and opinion of how well working fulltime combines with parenting and taking time for your marriage.

It all works, but it works at a cost. And you have to realize what the cost is. If you give your attention to one thing, it's a known fact that you're taking it away from something else. Sure, you have to try to keep balance in your life, but I think it's self-delusion if you tell yourself that you're doing all things equally well. For instance, if on my day off I take time to brief myself on Lebanon, that is time that I am *not* reading to my five-year-old. You have to be aware and constantly rebalancing not to let some part of your life receive less attention than it should.

Isn't "quality time" with your children enough?

I'm not sure. With the commuting schedule I had four days at home — days when I was not working. The children had almost *all* of my time on those days. I was gone three days on the weekend, but they had their father then and even their grandparents — I told myself that this really was okay.

For the first couple of years, they didn't seem to mind, but then I was put under a great deal of pressure from my children to give up the commute. What they said was that they wanted me *home*. Intellectually, it didn't make sense. I had concentrated, quality time with them when I was home. But they didn't see it that way. It was important to them that I was here in Denver *all* seven days.

In my job now, my hours are 12 noon until 7 in the evening. Even though I am gone three or four hours after they get home from school, they like that better than me being gone every weekend. If they wander into my bedroom in the middle of the night, I am there.

So you started to feel some guilt about being away?

Yes. I think stress and guilt are the two big pitfalls for a woman who works and has children. The guilt may come in a smaller dose if you absolutely have to work for financial reasons. If work is not an option, but a necessity, your *stress* level remains high, but your *guilt* may be lower. You know you have no choice.

My own mother worked not so much for self-fulfillment, but so her children could have economic advantages. She was fulfilling what she saw as her family's needs first. But — and I know this is a privilege — I am working not because I have to, to survive financially, but because I have to feel I've really used the skills I've developed.

A friend of mine, Marilyn Van Derbur Atler (a former Miss America who now runs the Motivational Institute Inc.), told me once, "Reynelda, I wouldn't be any better a mother if I were home fulltime." I think that's true for me, too.

Still, there is always the balance — the juggling. There's an internal guilt detector that goes off in me. When I start to feel guilty, the sirens start blaring and the lights go off. Then I know I have to do something. I will start cutting some other outside responsibilities or leave out some things I'd like to do for myself.

For instance, I resigned from the board of Rocky Mountain Women's Institute. I hated to, but I had to. I didn't have time to attend the meetings and take care of things at home. I wanted to take piano lessons. I took them for a few months, but they were taking a lot of time and I didn't want to feel guilty about it.

Do you have household help now?

Yes, and this is one thing I don't feel guilty about. If there is any way to finagle household help into your budget, do it. Someone cleans my house once a week. Before, I would come home, and the house would be a mess. I'd want to sit down and read a book, but I just couldn't do it. It was so overwhelming — and I had so much to do, especially when the children were small.

The question was *where* to start. I would sit here and feel like screaming or sucking my thumb! I didn't know whether to start in with the laundry, with the bedrooms, with the kitchen . . . .

So, I got help. I learned it was okay to delegate work. It makes me feel good when I come in to my house and it's halfway straight. When I would come home to my private space and find chaos, that would make me angry.

How do you and Daniel find time for yourselves?

It takes a lot of planning. We just have to sit down and say, we're going to take this time next Wednesday or whenever for ourselves. We both like to do a lot of family-oriented activities, but sometimes it's best if just the two of us get out together. You can't ignore, you have to spend time nourishing a marriage, too. In the years I commuted, we had no weekends together. It was hard, even though we did things during the week. I really think, again, that there is a price paid.

Any regrets about your time at Cable News Network?

No, I don't think so. The job forced me to grow. Professionally, I had to learn how to think on my feet more. I had to learn how to ad lib myself out of difficult situations. Very rarely does the anchor of a local newscast have to deal with as many unexpected things as I had to at CNN.

If news broke, we had to respond immediately. I was on the air when the marine compound in Beirut was blown up. Suddenly, I was faced with interviewing the Syrian ambassador to the United Nations, the Israeli ambassador to the United Nations, the Arab experts — all with absolutely no time to do any homework or any research. In the midst of this tragedy, all I could bring to the situation was anything I happened to remember or had read. Siutations like that have forced me to dig deeper inside myself.

How did Daniel handle your commuting?

Daniel had to learn how to manage the household — how to cook, how to work out the logistics with the kids. It was difficult at first, but I think he would say it was positive.

He had never cooked before. He's turned into an excellent cook. I would come home sometimes and the house would be filled with a wonderful aroma, and I'd ask, "What did you make?" He'd say, "I made your vegetarian loaf." Then I'd taste it, but it didn't taste like my recipe. "What did you do different?" I'd ask him. "Oh" he'd say, "I don't know. I just added this, that, and the other . . ." For awhile I went through a period of being a little bit jealous. But that passed! Daniel learned how to manage his time well and how to take care of everything. He really knows our kids. The kids see him both as a provider and a nurturer. He knows how to focus in on them and to listen to them, and how to sense what they're thinking and how they're doing.

You seem so intent on balancing your life. Do you meet any women who are extremely single-minded about their careers?

Yes — but they're usually not mothers. All the working mothers I see are racked by very painful choices at every step of the way.

The most ambitious women I meet today are choosing not to have kids. I meet quite a few couples who do not want children. They say, "We like our lifestyle. We like to have our time and money totally available for whatever we want to do." I respect that honesty. If a woman, or a couple, is not interested in sharing their lives with children, it's much better that they make this choice.

Allison St. Claire: Being a Single Parent

At the tender age of three and a half, Allison St. Claire marched into her hometown library in Columbus, Ohio, to request a library card. After signing her name in cursive, she got one.

Still a bibliophile, the forty-two-year-old managing editor of *Senior Edition* and *Colorado Old Times* in Denver, has also become an expert wordsmith. Yet, in our interview about her life as a single parent, this articulate woman leaves out all the obvious adjectives, never once describing herself as "worried, frazzled, or frustrated." She emphasizes instead the fun and the challenges of raising her fifteen-year-old son, Jason, and the sadness she feels thinking about how nearly grown up he is.

St. Claire has been divorced since Jason was three. The two of them live with four cats, two dogs, fourteen fish, and one gerbil, in a sturdy 1915 bungalow in Denver's Park Hill neighborhood.

St. Clarie hates housework. If she were not the conservationist she is — bundled newspapers are stacked on the front porch beside sacks of crushed aluminum cans — she would resort to using paper plates. Instead, dishes soak in the sink. Floors need vacuuming. Furniture needs dusting. But other things have a higher priority. Jason. Her job. Reading. Gardening. Weekend trips to the mountains. Household projects.

"The projects around here aren't like housework," St. Claire explains. "They're fun! And they give me a sense of competence and self-sufficiency." Recently, with the help of an adult friend, she and Jason built and installed a satellite dish. Their latest mother-son project is the addition of a passive solar greenhouse to the house's sunny south side.

Because St. Claire is the most relaxed and happy single parent I have encountered, and because Jason is an easy-going adolescent who by all indications is growing into an independent and happy young man, I wanted to hear more about her parenting experiences.

St. Claire pours white wine, while Calamity, her solid black cat, chooses my lap to purr in while we talk over dinner. She serves a delicious vegetarian squash spaghetti with herb tomato and a green salad. She has worked all day, prepared dinner, and has brought home more work to complete after we finish.

She is frank and informal. Her laugh is hearty. As it spills out, it reminds me of a waterfall tumbling into a deep reservoir.

Conversations

Tell me about you and Jason.

My husband and I adopted Jason when he was four months old. We were school teachers in Jefferson County (in suburban Denver). Soon, we found we both wanted more time with Jason, so we tried convincing the county to let us share *one* teaching job. They refused, so we both quit.

What we ended up doing was driving a cab. We could share one cab. I drove some days while Al drove others. We took Jason along with us some of the time, and this job-sharing worked out well.

Also, we were living in a communal situation. This meant we had one to three other adults around most of the time. I think I am an adequate single parent in part because I have been really delighted to share my son with other significant adults.

Back during those early years, I could come home from driving the cab, feeling really rotten — or my husband could come home exhausted, but Jason didn't have to relate just to one of us. He had other caring adults to whom he could go.

One of these women, Tara Bartee, who lived with us then, had made a decision not to have her own children, but she felt deeply involved with Jason. She made a commitment then to help parent Jason, and even now she continues that involvement. We live separately, but she still has Jason over to her house one or two days a week.

Once, when Jason was in preschool, a teacher asked, "Who is in your family?" He answered, "I have a mom, a dad, and a Tara." He didn't call her "Auntie" Tara, as she might have been called twenty-five years ago, because she is much more than that. Today Jason really does not have me as a *single* parent. He is with Tara or over at his dad's house a couple of days a week.

But still — isn't it hard being the primary parent yourself?

I'm going to reveal one of my deepest, most intimate secrets. (She laughs.) I am delighted to do it alone. It's a lot easier!

I have lots of opinions about how things ought to be done, and I don't especially like to have to spend time explaining my position or working it out with a second person. I *like* making the decisions.

I think one of the most revealing moments of my life came when Jason was around seven years old, and I had been on my own for three years. I was driving down the street thinking about the plans I was making for a trip that Jason and I were going to take. And then it hit me that I was doing all the things my father did in my family — making money, making decisions, planning a trip, driving on trips — it felt really good to be doing all that.

And then I realized that I was also making the decisions that my mother used to make. *That* was really nice to realize, too. It seemed like somehow I had gotten the best from both of them and had incorporated it all into myself!

When I was growing up, I knew just one kind of woman. She was a housewife, and she was married, and that was all. One neighbor down the street had a job, but that was so mysterious. It was as if we didn't talk about those people, because a woman's place on earth was to get married, have children, and stay home with them all the time. That's fine as an option — I just want Jason to know that women come in as many varieties as men do and that people can be androgynous in the best sense.

But making all the decisions is not that easy, is it?

No! About a year after I was divorced, my dog became sick and needed to be put away — she was very old. But facing that decision, I wanted somebody — anybody — to say it was an "okay" idea. But I was totally responsible. I had to do it — arrange with the vet, drive the dog over. . . . Getting through that made it easier to be responsible for my decisions.

Bearing consequences is one of the ways people grow. If I make a good decision, I get to enjoy all the rewards. I can say to myself, "Hey, you are a *smart* lady." If I make a bad decision, I can say, "You 'dumb-dumb,' don't do that again."

Was there any special reason you decided to adopt a child?

Somehow I never felt the need to biologically reproduce myself. But I felt I could be a swell parent, and that I would love to offer whatever it was that parents offer a kid. It really didn't matter *which* kid. Just give me one, I thought, and let me play with it for the next eighteen years!

Back when I was deciding to adopt, I would find people who'd say, "I couldn't raise a child who's not my own blood." That astounded me. They seemed to be selfish about what *kind* of child they wanted. It was as though they needed a replica of their own egos instead of a new soul they could nurture and appreciate as it grew and flowered.

In combining your career and parenting, what is the biggest challenge for you right now?

Not to let my anxiety level run amok. If I can't figure out where to get the money to buy Jason the new pair of boots he needs, then sitting around worrying isn't going to do it.

I have found that if I write a problem down, that helps get it out of my mind and into my life. By writing it down, I'm saying, "I'll worry about this when it's appropriate." When I discipline myself to do this, it helps. For example, if when I'm leaving the office at six o'clock at night, and all of a sudden I remember something I've got to do tomorrow, I'll just take five extra minutes to write it down. *Then* I can leave it on my desk. I don't have to carry it home in my head.

As for raising Jason — and in handling any human relationship — I think the real challenge is sorting out what the real issue is. When he is upset or sad, what does he really mean? A while back he began complaining that I was gone too much. He was not being deprived of meals, or of transportation to a school event, or any of the mechanical things I could think of. He was saying, I think, that he needed more attention.

So I made sure that when I came home from work, there was time specifically devoted to him — exclusively devoted to him. If the dishes needed washing, tough. If the laundry needed doing, too bad. I hope I was responding to what he really was saying.

Then, and for me, most of the time, attention to the house is last. When is housekeeping really more important than sitting down and playing a game with my son? There's no contest. That child's in my life for eighteen years only, and God knows, I'll have dishes to do the rest of my life. And even with Jason grown, with a little luck, I'll still find better things to do!

Is there anything you like to do just for yourself?

Periodically, I'll take a night class in something I'm interested in. That's about all right now. I'm not even dating. Even the logistics of a relationship seem too complicated and overwhelming. I *might* be ready for a once-a-week relationship — going out to the movies or for a drink. But I find myself deliberately cutting myself off from the places where I know there are interesting people to meet.

All of a sudden, it's like, "Oh God, that would be one more detail in my life." Is the trade-off for having some companionship worth it? That's an issue I'm dealing with at this point. Right now I'm focusing on my career and on Jason. Other things have temporarily fallen by the wayside. It's an intermission, perhaps. Later, who knows?

What values have you tried to teach Jason?

I would hope I have taught him consideration for others. That boils down to accepting the Quaker precept that there is "that of God" in every person. (She stops, then laughs.) I grew up saying *man*, but I like saying person instead. (St. Claire holds a B.S. in Spanish and education from Earlham College, a Quaker school, and an M.A. in Latin American history from the University of Maryland.)

Quakers are pacifists. If you believe, as they do, that God is in every person, that God is in all of us and in every thing, then you don't go out and hurt another human being. You don't go out and destroy the earth.

I'm a pantheist, too. I have tried to teach Jason respect for the earth's resources. It's not okay to trample a flower. God is among the trees and rocks and flowers, too, I believe. (St. Claire, her brother, and a friend have recently formed a company to convert city sludge into biologically alive organic compost.)

I also want Jason to be self-sufficient, like my grandparents. They were intellectuals — readers and seekers. Yet they were also doers. They were balanced people with many interests. I would wish that balance for Jason.

He has helped build the greenhouse and satellite dish. He helps in the garden. He knows how to work the computer we got last year. He can change the oil in the car.

My parents wanted me to enter a profession, so it took me a long time to learn all these practical matters. I like seeing Jason learning to work with his hands *and* his head.

What advice would you have for other single parents?

This would apply to single or "double" parents. Feel good about your parenting. And if you don't feel good about the way you're doing it, now is the time to step back and examine what you're doing — to find out why you don't think it's working out, and to get help if necessary.

I want to keep on loving Jason for who he is, and to help him become the person he wants to be. My intent has always been to raise a loving, independent child, one who knows something about the resources in this world and how to use them appropriately.

It feels good to see Jason growing up. It feels sad. It's one of those paradoxes in life. I realize that I've grown dependent on Jason. I won't be bereft when he's grown, but I'll miss him. He's the only person I know who can assemble something without even having to read the directions. I've taught him some things, but that skill is something he just can't seem to pass on to me!

(Jason joins us near the end of our conversation. He is friendly, at ease, but not eager to be asked questions. But he does consent to answering two.)

What's the best thing about having your mom as a parent?

She's not as strict as most of my friends' parents! But she does like to know where I am. Last week I forgot and didn't leave her a note when I went out after school. She just told me not to do that again. I'm leaving notes now.

What's her weakest point in parenting?

Maybe letting me do what I want to, too much!

(Realizing he has picked her lack of strictness as both her strongest and weakest parental trait, Jason and St. Claire share an understanding laugh).

Pat Schroeder: In the House and at Home

Congresswoman Pat Schroeder meets me at her Denver condominium on a spring Saturday afternoon. Five days a week she juggles legislative responsibilities in Washington. Then, almost every weekend, she flies to Denver to mingle with constituents.

Despite her constant traveling, she radiates an intense energy and there are no circles under her clear hazel eyes. She is dressed fashionably in an understated outfit, her brown tweed jacket accented with an ERA pin stuck decisively through the lapel. Her suede pumps have heels low enough for easy walking.

Already she has spoken at a banquet honoring women in the work force and has dropped in at the botanical gardens for a neighborhood talent show. After this, more community events follow.

Though Sally Brown, Schroeder's longtime Denver aide, reminds her of the afternoon's agenda and prods her to keep moving, Schroeder insists on microwaving popcorn before we seat ourselves around her dining room table on patriotic Hitchcock chairs decorated with golden eagles and the nation's Capitol.

Drinking pop and munching popcorn with this gracious woman, it is hard to imagine her as the tough, strong politician some have reportedly characterized as a "pushy broad." An *Esquire* article, "The Political Woman's Long, Hard Climb," by Nicholas von Hoffman reports her reputation thus, but lists no source. Apparently, however, some of the other House members do see her this way.

"They'd prefer it if we (women) stuck to National Women's History Week," Schroeder says in that same article. "My colleagues say that I've lost my femininity, but at some point you have to choose up sides, make them vote on it. I think I've been effective. I've gotten 'em angry."

That Schroeder is a complex mixture of the yin and the yang, the masculine and the feminine, is apparent. About her, Brown says simply, "She has many facets, and that tends to scare some people." But person to person, off the House floor, she is softer than harsh black-and-white wire photos reflect, and more charming than a quick appearance on a television news report indicates.

Schroeder's comfortable condominium is compact and not lavish in any way. On one wall rests an antique baby carriage, and across from it, covering the red brick wall which extends from the dining area into the kitchen, are all sorts of nostalgic relics — an old horse collar, a washboard, a cowbell, flour sacks.

That the liberal democratic feminist lawmaker collects such whimsical decorative accents is somehow surprising. An old arcade game, a "Photo Fortune Telling" machine, promises to spit out a picture of your future career if you insert a penny. Schroeder, of course, did not leave her career choice to chance.

When she was growing up, she wanted to be a ballerina, but at eleven, already towering over her mother, she decided she was too tall and awkward. Later, after soloing in a light plane in 1959, she considered becoming a commercial pilot, but poor eyesight stopped her. Toward the end of her undergraduate work in college, she began to think about going on to law school.

Despite college counselors who could not understand her drive and her mother's misgiving that she might forego marriage and never produce any grandchildren, Schroeder applied to law school. After graduating magna cum laude and Phi Beta Kappa from the University of Minnesota in just three years, she entered Harvard Law School in 1961.

As it turned out, her mother need not have worried — at Harvard, she met and married fellow law student Jim Schroeder. And they did have children — Scott and Jamie.

In 1972, when Schroeder was first elected to Congress, as a Democrat representing Denver's 1st Congressional District, Scott was a first-grader. Daughter Jamie was only two. Schroeder, who can smile about it now, remembers (as reported in *ElectriCity*, May 1984) being the only person "ever sworn into Congress clutching a handbag filled with disposable diapers." Now, she is both the senior member of the Colorado congressional delegation and the senior female House member.

From where we sit, I can see a small decorative slab of granite on her kitchen counter inscribed, "You never hear of a man being asked how he manages to combine marriage with a career." Since I have come expressly for the purpose of asking Schroeder how she manages, I apologize for needing to ask.

Schroeder, the realist, assures me she does not mind, but, "yes," she laughs, "I do hope the curiosity about how women do both will dwindle someday." Meanwhile, as one of twenty-three women out of 435 in the House of Representatives, she well knows that this day has not arrived.

In the Schroeders' living room, two framed photographs are side by side on a table. In one, the family stands on a high Colorado mountain trail with a panorama of peaks spread behind them. In the other, arms linked, the four of them smile widely with the nation's Capitol a backdrop.

How has Pat Schroeder inhabited these two worlds while keeping both her family and career intact? Like her now-famous signature with its smiling face in the middle of a sweeping "P", she smiles, too, as she explains.

Conversations

When you were first elected, when both children were so young, were you concerned about being able to handle both a family and a legislative career?

Absolutely! Even knowing that I generally accomplish what I set out to do, there was something — not in my head, but in my stomach — that said, "What are you doing? Have you lost your mind?"

It was really refreshing to find out that my fears were unfounded. It has all worked, the family has held together very well.

When we were out for dinner the other night, my daughter was saying that so many of her friends have families whose lives are like a soap opera. Because of my career, we're supposed to be the unstable ones, but we're still together. I think it may be because each family member is into what is important for him or her, and none of us has restricted or held back the others.

You manage to stay calm. How?

(Sally Brown breaks into laughter and answers.) Well, we have a thing called the Duck Club . . .

(Schroeder takes over.) My father always used to say, "The trick is to get through life like a swan. Above the water you look as if you're calm, but underneath, you're paddling like mad." Every now and then Sally will say, "Hey, Pat! Your feet are showing!"

Staying calm is just one goal. Another is remaining "real." If you're not careful, in politics you can get so hung up with your image that you lose touch with reality. As a politician, it's easy to become more and more self-focused, to start thinking that everybody should fit into your universe.

But families usually don't let a mother off the hook as easily as a father. So even if people are handing me coffee, opening my door, putting the keys in my hand, or even driving me around — in other words, catering to my needs all day — when I go home, someone reminds me it's my night to do the dishes.

Part of the reason our family works may be because I still do my part, so they feel more conscientious about doing theirs, too.

How have you been able to prioritize your life so effectively?

I have tried to learn to understand what really matters. Years ago I stayed up late one night baking a cake for a cake sale at Scott's school. I felt sorry for myself, but I was determined to stay up and finish that cake. Well, the next day Scott came home, not thanking me, but saying some of the kids had just brought money.

I realized then that it was the contribution he needed, not my sacrifice in time. At that point I stopped and asked myself, "Why am I doing this?" There are so many things like this. We keep on doing things from tradition or because someone has told us we must. But finally we need to sit down and talk to our children and husbands. When I did this, I found out they didn't care really if I continued doing all the traditional things as long as I cared about what they were doing and as long as we took time out to do some things together.

What is your greatest personal satisfaction right now?

It's that my kids are doing so fantastically well. They have added an incredible amount to my life.

We've raised them to have self-respect and confidence — they're not hot house plants. They know how to take care of themselves. Even if I couldn't get home for dinner, I know Scott could drive someplace and get groceries or pick up something from a restaurant. Before he drove, he and Jamie used to call Yellow Cab and go out to eat. We got to be good friends with the cab company back then.

How do you keep in touch with your kids, staying as busy as you do?

Jim and I communicate to the children how important they are in our lives. Everybody in the family feels totally free to intercede, too, to present complaints or concerns when they need to. We try and squeeze in as much time together as we possibly can. Sometimes Jamie and Scott come down to the office to do their homework. I also take them along with me on trips.

The children come to Denver with me often, but they just "hit the place" and go off skiing — like the other people flying out here from Washington. I don't bring my skis! I get off the plane and have office appointments, speeches, dropping by banquets. It's not fair!

What is your home in Virginia like?

We live in Alexandria, Virginia, in the least fancy house in the delegation. People assume we have a house like the governor has. When guests come for dinner, you can see by the looks on their faces that they are thinking, "This isn't any different from my house."

We bought the house just after I won the first time. No one thought I would win, and when I did, there was no time to spend on house hunting. Jim was practicing law. The children were just two and six.

We called a realtor and told her what we needed. When she found a house, we took it, thinking we wouldn't be there very long. We even ordered the carpeting over the phone. They had red in stock and we needed it quickly, so that's the color we got.

Well, we're still there. Every now and then someone in the family says something about moving, and I say, "Fine, you go and find something else." The response is a rather quick, "Oh, no, no!"

What this family needs is a "wife." If we had a "wife," we'd go find another house.

What has Jim's role been through the years?

He has been terrific! There are people who try and portray him as a "house husband," however, and he certainly is *not* that. He has a busy law practice.

Do you divide up chores?

Everybody in our family pitches in and does something. We have no role assignments. Everybody is supposed to do what they can do when they find the time.

If Jim is home, and I am away, he manages the house. He makes sure there is enough food and that there are clean clothes. If I'm home and he is away, I'll do that. If we're both home, we decide who does what, based on what each of us is doing that particular week.

It just does not work for us to have fixed chores — charts and lists. No one *always* unloads the dishwasher or *always* washes the clothes. I know some people couldn't live like this. But we find that the household runs more smoothly if we just see what needs to be done every day, talk over who does it, and then get busy!

How our house looks is not a top priority. We've tried to put our family relationships first.

How do you unwind when you get a spare moment?

I just try not to get "wound." If you basically enjoy what you're doing, you learn to do it without getting all uptight. If lyou try to compartmentalize your life, this can lead to tension.

If I say, now is "rest" time, now is "work" time, now is "my" time, now is "their" time, then I'd go nuts trying to figure out whose time it is.

I don't take lots of time off. I try to stay relaxed as mfuch as possible all the time.

If you were suddenly given a day off, what would you do?

That depends. I love kite flying in Colorado in the spring. Or if it's summer, I might just roam around in the mountains. Anytime, I would like just being able to sit and read. It seems as if I've got twenty piles of books lying around. I hate to tell you how many first chapters I've read.

(The one book Schroeder has finished? *The Butter Battle Book* by Dr. Seuss. The children's book is about a fight between two groups — one who butters their bread butter side up, and the other who butters theirs butter side down. They feel compelled to go to war over this difference. The volume is Dr. Seuss' protest against the nuclear arms race. Schroeder shares Dr. Seuss' view on this issue.)

What are your goals for the future?

Just to keep on. I figure that much of the population goes to bed every night bored with their routines, but that's the last thing I can say. The days are *not* dull. But I'm on this treadmill, and if I ever decided it didn't work, or if I tried to get off, then maybe I might set women back.

Would people say, "Well, we had a woman in the House, but she didn't stay with it?" I feel I carry around a lot of responsibility. I think about that a lot.

Do you think women often fail to reach their potentials?

Many do. We tend to be afraid to take risks. But if we want to contribute something in any field — politics, medicine, law, business, the arts, volunteer work, any endeavor — then we just need to go ahead and do it. We need to look for *how* we can go ahead, not *why* we can't.

I feel gratitude toward the women who have gone before me — women like Harriet Tubman and Eleanor Roosevelt. Just knowing that they dared to contribute to their worlds, in their own ways, makes me feel a kinship with them.

So you feel you are a role model for other women?

I really hope so. I hope it won't be so hard for the next generation of women. I think of the bright, well-educated counselors I had in college who said, "Now why do you want to go on to law school, honey?" If your counselors are telling you to trim your sails and not to aim that high . . . it really breaks my heart to look back on that.

Yes, I do hope women will say, "If she can do it, I can do it." When I grew up I didn't know any congresswomen, there were so few back then. There were almost none.

Frank Shorter: Redefining the Rules

In 1969, after graduating from Yale, where he was all-American in track, Frank Shorter wondered what might happen if he devoted an entire year to training. How much faster could he run? How much better might he become? If he did not find out, might he wake up some day, middle-aged, wondering?

Not willing to face any lingering "what if's," Shorter began an intense year of training, basing himself in Florida during the fall and winter of 1969 to 1970 and moving on to the cooler high country in Colorado that summer.

"I experimented, tested myself, ran a little faster, a little longer; everything I did was consistent with the need to get the most out of my running ability," he wrote, remembering this period (from *Olympic Gold: A Runner's Life and Times* by Frank Shorter, with Marc Bloom, Houghton Mifflin Company, Boston, 1984).

As it turned out, his efforts earned him a place in sports history. In Munich in 1972, he became the first American to capture an Olympic gold medal in the marathon since 1908. In the 1976 Montreal Olympics, he won the silver medal.

"We have no greater example of the runner than Frank Shorter," writes Marc Bloom. The late James F. Fixx, best-selling author of *The Complete Book of Running,* credited Shorter with laying the groundwork for the running boom.

Fatherly duties having nothing to do with running or fame have made Shorter a few minutes late the day we talk. He arrives at his sportswear company in Boulder, Colorado, wearing a sweatshirt and sweatpants and apologizing because lunch with his young son Mark took longer than he had planned.

Our conversation takes place in Shorter's office, a large room which holds just enough dust and disarray to make a visitor feel at ease. A child-sized desk fills one corner. A pair of running shoes rests on his desktop. From a coatrack droops an assortment of running shorts, shirts, and socks. Taped slightly crooked on one wall is a construction paper "thank you" crayoned with a brilliant rainbow. Shorter explains that a sixth-grade class to which he recently spoke sent him this.

At the age of forty, Shorter still has a runner's lean frame. He still runs every day and he enters ten or twelve races a year, ranging from one- to three-mile fun runs to 10K (6.2-mile) and marathon events.

Shorter, who has a law degree from the University of Florida, also remains involved in Frank Shorter Sportswear, the wholesale clothing company that he founded. In addition, he is a sports commentator for NBC and a contributing editor for *Runner's World* magazine, and he has appeared in commercials for United Airlines, Canon Camera, and Sanyo Video Products.

Since his Olympic successes, Frank Shorter has remained an amateur runner. To strip him of amateur status would have been like caging an eagle as far as he was concerned. There are rules against professional runners signing up for amateur races, and Shorter wanted to be able to run in amateur races everywhere, all over the country.

Yet, at the same time, even with a law degree and other possible career options, Shorter also wanted to make a living in some enterprise related to running. "The question became, how can I make my living like this, yet remain amateur," he explains.

Here Shorter tells about his part in helping to redefine amateur sports in this country so that amateurs now have more latitude in earning money from their particular sport. He also shares his thoughts about keeping a perspective on the success and fame which began with a commitment to training close to twenty years ago.

He does not seem impressed with himself or his achievements as he talks. He is intense, a little shy, and, I suspect, most at ease when he is by himself, running.

Conversations

Did you dream of being famous when you first ran in the Olympic marathon in 1972?

No. My motivation for running in the Olympics wasn't financial, and it wasn't recognition — it was simply to do well in the event. When I started out running, long-distance runners were odd-balls. They were weird guys with long hair who spoke a funny language. My doing well in the Olympics happened to coincide with the beginning of the running boom. Now the language of runners may still seem funny to some people, and some people still think runners are strange, masochistic people, but almost everybody understands running terms and jargon.

Was it tempting to "sell" yourself after winning the gold medal?

Not really. In 1972, I watched Mark Spitz, a champion Olympic swimmer. He had lawyers, accountants, and advertising agencies carefully orchestrating his life. At that time that was the standard way to go when you won the gold medal — hire an agent, send out 8 x 10 glossies, and sell yourself to Madison Avenue. I decided to do it differently.

I thought to myself, yes, it would be nice to capitalize on my name and success, but why not do it in a way that not only benefited me but somehow had a tangible impact on the sport and others. By staying amateur, I could not only keep running, but make a living and perhaps change my sport for the better.

Change the sport in what way?

In the early 1970s, rules were being implemented and interpreted in much the same way as they had been since the British aristocracy created them before the turn of the century. These rules of amateur eligibility were right for their time, but they did not work for modern athletes.

Until recently, athletes in track and field and other Olympic sports have had an extremely difficult time achieving excellence in this country. Athletes could earn absolutely no pay from anything connected to their field of excellence. As was inevitable, some took money anyway in a shady, underground system of payoffs. And those who did not usually had to work at fulltime jobs. There is no way to achieve real excellence in a sport while working at something else all day.

Jim Thorpe was the most famous athlete denied his amateur status over issues like this. His decathlon and pentathlon titles from the

Stockholm Olympics of 1912 were taken from him after it was learned that he had earned a few dollars in professional baseball. It took seventy years for the International Olympic Committee to overturn that decision.

And who makes the rules?

The International Amateur Athletic Federation (IAAF) is the world governing body for track and field and running. Every Olympic sport has such a body, and all of them are recognized by the International Olympic Committee (IOC).

The International Olympic Committee offers broad guidelines which these world governing bodies follow. But it is the governing bodies themselves that make the rules for each of their sports and are responsible for seeing that they are followed.

But it is even more complex than this. Every world governing body, such as the IAAF, has, in turn, member federations, or national governing bodies in virtually every nation. And these national level bodies are supposed to enforce the international rules in every country.

The Amateur Athletic Union (AAU) was the national governing body for track and field and running in the United States. Then, in 1978, that body became The Athletics Congress (TAC). The AAU had always been terribly restrictive and extremely strict about what an amateur could do.

How did you get involved in trying to change these rules?

In the summer of 1975, I was asked to testify at a congressional hearing of the President's Commission on Olympic Sports. Its stated mission was "to determine what factors impede or tend to impede the United States from fielding its best teams in international competition."

On September 9, 1975, I was the last of four Olympic athletes to testify, and I chose to be quite direct. I said than an Olympic-caliber athlete could not work fulltime and be expected to maintain his form, much less improve. I added that the United States could no longer impose its standards of amateurism on the rest of the world and that most countries were subsidizing their athletes. I pointed out that we were one of the few pristine nations left. (The rules that Shorter desired to change were international ones. Most countries had already gone ahead and interpreted them in a more liberal way to benefit their national amateur athletes.)

When I was asked hypothetically what I might have expected to receive from my country had I been a Russian returning with a gold medal from the 1972 Olympic marathon, instead of an American athlete, I answered, "I would rather have been a Finn. Had I been a Finn, my hometown might have given me a free house, all of this tax-free, and I could have done endorsements. Every time I would have gone to a shopping center, I would have gotten two thousand dollars for cutting a ribbon. I could have demanded two thousand dollars every time I set foot on the track for the rest of the summer and probably all of the rest of the next year" (from *Olympic Gold: A Runner's Life and Times*).

Then they asked me what I got as an American. And this was my answer: "You know, I haven't even gotten my Olympic ring from the Olympic Committee yet."

I had stirred things up with this testimony and there seemed to be a good possibility that my amateur status might be challenged. The IAAF asked the AAU for a clarification of my testimony. They were upset. In a way, I had embarrassed them by exposing the differences in the ways amateurs were treated in various countries. I knew that they might be angry enough to strip me of my amateur standing.

I went back to the people at the President's Commission and asked them for help. They really gave me no support. The commission had a noble mission, but it looked as if they might be willing to use me as a martyr for the cause. They were not going to defend me.

Fortunately, my testimony had not been sworn under oath. I reviewed my testimony and refined my remarks, putting them in the form of a deposition. I submitted this to the AAU and waited. Finally, I received word from the AAU in January 1976 that they were satisfied that I had not violated my amateur status. They forwarded their opinion to the IAAF, and finally—seven months before the 1976 Olympics, I was a reconfirmed amateur. In effect, I was forgiven for speaking so recklessly. The AAU (now the Athletics Congress) had paved the way for changing amateur rules in this country.

But when did the rules actually begin to be reinterpreted?

Finally after the 1976 Olympics. That year the IAAF approved my opening a Frank Shorter Sports Store with my name on it. Then, in 1977, I started manufacturing Frank Shorter Running Gear. Again, the IAAF gave its permission.

There were stipulations in both these instances, of course. I could not just be promoting the store or the running apparel. I was required to be active in the businesses and would have to own at least 51 percent of each concern.

Another change occurred in 1977. I began doing clinics at races. This was probably the single most important step in the reform of amateurism and in the running movement in general in the 1970s. Again, the rules were redefined. A runner could promote events and share what he or she knew about running without turning "professional."

In 1979, I was asked to become a Hilton International employee. I would be paid by Hilton for my services as a consultant. Hilton proposed paying TAC (the newly formed national governing body, the Athletics Congress) $25,000 a year for the right to use one of their athletes — me — in their promotions. When this was approved, another avenue of earnings opened up for amateur athletes.

Finally, in December 1981, a new trust fund system was set up for athletes. At last, an athlete could accept appearance or prize money at a competition as long as the money was withdrawn only for legitimate training expenses. This money can be withdrawn for education, living, travel — but the corpus, the bulk of the trust, must remain there until the athlete turns professional. Still, the money is the athlete's. There just is no access to all of it until the official act of turning professional takes place. Now finally, our athletes can be supported in much the same way an eastern European athlete is supported by his or her country. Now there will be fewer aspiring Olympic athletes surviving on food stamps! (As Shorter did during his training period in 1970.)

You don't seem to have let all you've accomplished "go to your head." How have you avoided that?

You're in real trouble when you start believing what people say about you. I'm basically introverted, so I spend a lot of time by myself. For the two or three hours a day I'm out running, I try and set things in perspective. I try to make sure I have a hold on what's going on.

I don't want to burn out, you know, go on the grand tour, hit thirty cities in ten weeks, make money, cash in while I can. I would rather be reasonable about my personal and financial expectations, and hope that my lifestyle, which I really enjoy, can continue for as long a period as possible.

I don't feel the way some professional athletes do — that eventually I'll have to sit down. I see my running as a kind of evolution. As I get older, I'm not going to the Olympics, but I just became a masters runner. I tend to think long-term.

But you enjoy your public life — your appearances?

Being out in public is fun, but it's important to remember that you see the very good sides of people in these situations. Who knows whether the person who's being so nice to you doesn't go home and beat his wife? That's an extreme example, but you have to realize that part of the pleasure you get from being in public is in bringing out the best in people, in making them happy — in satisfying their curiosity, in providing them with information they want.

At the same time, people are seeing the public part of you. You hope all this is helpful. It is enjoyable. But it is all surface. In other words, people I meet are putting their best foot forward, just as I am. But life is so much more than this.

Is it hard going from these public appearances back into your private life?

When my kids, Mark and Alex, look at me, I'm "Daddy." That's who I am. In trying to be a good parent, in maintaining a handle on "success," in the end it really is a question of making sure you don't believe everything people say.

Success can be so arbitrary. I'm successful based on an arbitrary distance. If the distance had been twenty miles rather than twenty-six miles that particular day in 1972, I might not have been the best.

Some people worry that suddenly one day their success will be gone. My attitude has always been to act in a manner that will minimize the impact of that day. In other words, if I woke up tomorrow and all my running ability was gone and nobody wanted to see me race anymore or listen to me in a running clinic — I could do television work. I could pursue business activities. When your talent is ebbing, go ahead and diversify. It's the best insurance.

What are your priorities right now?

My family, my running, and my business, probably in that order. Business is tertiary to what I do — but I'm lucky. Most people don't have the luxury of that choice because money comes first. Otherwise they don't eat.

(Shorter pauses. I have finished my questions, but wonder if a dramatic painting that hangs behind this desk has any special significance. It is a monochromatic canvas of a rowboat which is beached. The shadow of a gull looms overhead.)

Could you tell me about that painting?

It's by Andrew Wyeth. I met Wyeth and saw that boat as the picture was being painted. In prep school, Steve Cook, my roommate from Maine, happened to be Wyeth's nephew. When I was up in Maine visiting my friend, we went over to Wyeth's house.

Wyeth showed me this boat he was painting, and he said, "I'm painting this because earlier this summer, there was a lobster man out in his dory, and I saw this man fall out of the boat and drown."

Lobster men wear hip boots. And most don't learn how to swim, because they know if they fall in the water, they'll drown. You can't swim with hip boots on. If you fall into the water, you're dead.

This painting always reminds me that I'm a different kind of person from that lobster man. I would be the kind of lobster man who would know how to swim — and I would invent some boots with zippers so that I could get them off if I fell in.

In a way, this painting reminds me that it's possible to change something and to survive in the process if you really want to.

Mo Siegel: Reaching Your Potential

Mo Siegel, the energetic president and founder of Celestial Seasonings, the herb tea company, swept into his Boulder plant out of breath. "I took a fast and furious ride to get here," he explained, still wearing the protective helmet he puts on when he bicycles to work — which is almost every day. "You've got to get aerobic, you know," he added, unbuckling the head gear and bending over to rip off the Velcro leg bands that protect pants from bicycle chains.

His reddish brown hair was tousled. His cheeks were still flushed from the cool March air, but Mo did not linger in the reception area. "Let's get started," he said, ushering me into his office, motioning me to be seated on the navy blue velvet sofa along one wall. After clearing his throat and stretching for a second, Mo quickly sank into the cushion next to me. He was ready to begin our interview. He is not a man who likes wasting time.

Mo grew up in Palmer Lake, Colorado. After graduating from Catholic prep school at seventeen, he enrolled at Western State College in Gunnison, Colorado. "I hated it, being cooped up in classes with my nose forced into a book," he later wrote in an article for *Guideposts* magazine. "I didn't have four years to become formally educated. Life was calling, opportunities waiting. Education would have to be self-taught."

After only two months, Mo dropped out, trying a variety of jobs — running a health food store in Aspen, Colorado, working on a fishing trawler off the Florida coast. Then, in 1969, he came back to Colorado, this time settling in Boulder.

Mo has told the rest of the story in feature articles every place from *The Wall Street Journal* to *USA Today*. One day, as he remembers it, he was wandering through a mountain field "thick with different herbs and flowers." There, the Colorado native, who as a child had picked and sold wild berries, concocted an idea.

In the late 1960s, people were drinking herb teas such as peppermint, but as yet no one had marketed herb-tea mixtures. Mo, an avid tea drinker, decided to keep on mixing different herbs until he found a blend of complimentary flavors.

Mo hiked into the hills again and again, gathering different varieties of herbs into burlap sacks, stashing them in backpacks, and then trekking home to experiment. Finally, he sipped a blend with a taste he found just right. He called that tea, which contained thirty-six different herbs, "Mo's 36."

Mo's 36 sold to health food stores, but it was not until a large food distributor agreed to carry it that the small home enterprise became a full-fledged company. (At this point, a friend, John Hay, joined the company and remained with Celestial Seasonings until 1979.) The first batch of tea, shipped out in 1971, contained 10,000 tea bags — all in muslin bags that Mo's wife Peggy and John Hay's wife Beth had hand-sewn. Today, Celestial Seasonings annually sells three-quarters of a billion tea bags.

After that original mixture, others followed — Red Zinger, Mandarin Orange Spice, Emperor's Choice, to name a few of the better known. Besides acquainting the public with new tastes in tea, Celestial Seasonings also changed the way teas are packaged. From the beginning, they splashed their boxes with colorful artwork ranging from a sleeping bear in a nightcap to a rotund Chinese emperor holding a walking stick. And each box includes a touch of philosophy from quotables such as Abraham Lincoln and Mark Twain.

Mo was just twenty when he launched Celestial Seasonings. By the time he was twenty-six, he was a millionaire. In those early days, his hair was long and his jeans had peace symbols sewn over the worn spots. Today, his clothes have a neat, Ivy League flair, and his hair is shorter, though he sports a generous mustache.

In Mo's office a personal computer is stationed behind an executive-sized desk covered with piles of neatly stacked papers and samples of a new organic line of shampoos. Bookshelves are cluttered with everything from *A Child's Garden of Verses* to *In Search of Excellence*.

Two familiar paintings hang behind the sofa on which we sit. In one, a bear — the bear of the "Lemon Delight" box — drinks iced tea while reclining in a mountain pool beneath a waterfall. In the other, an old-fashioned shepherdess — from the "Spearmint" box — sits in a mountain meadow, her faithful dog at her feet, sheep surrounding her.

If you want to reach your human potential, how do you do it? In this comfortable setting, in quick staccato sentences, Mo addresses this subject. Like tea bags shooting off in an ultra-modern assembly line, his thoughts tumble out in rapid succession. Throughout our conversation, he has the enthusiasm of Richard Simmons, sprinkled with the otherworldly zaniness of Mork. Here is what Mo had to say.

Conversations

How do you think we can reach our potentials?

First determine what you want to do, and then go do it. Go after the goals you have chosen. But you need to set your goals *very clearly*! And remember, in setting goals, you also have to set priorities. You need to know how to prioritize and not try to do too many things. A person with seven goals is going to be more successful than a person with fifty.

I have a hard time imagining people who don't know what they want. But those who really don't know should just start *doing*. One way to start is to set some immediate goals instead of long-range ones.

If you want to be successful, you can't fear failure. If you're growing, you'll be stretching, and just inherent in the concept of stretching is failure. You learn as much from your failures as from your successes.

We all fail sometimes. For instance, we bought a field of the world's finest peppermint in 1974. It was in Wisconsin, and that year in Wisconsin the sun never came out and the frost hit, wiping out about a third of the crop. A third of that crop was almost all our profit.

We have to accept failures, but combined with that acceptance is learning, corporately as well as individually, to recognize the small successes. There are not as many quantum leaps as there are everyday small successes. Look for these along the way. Appreciate them, and reward yourself for them. As these small triumphs pile up, you'll start building a mindset that's conducive to success.

I think that approximately 85 percent of your objectives should be met every year. If you're only accomplishing 20 percent, maybe you're setting objectives that are too difficult. On the other hand, if you're accomplishing 100 percent every year, you haven't set goals that are hard enough. Figure this — 15 percent of the time you're not going to reach your objectives even when you set them correctly.

When things go wrong, it helps just to sit back and count your blessings. Norman Vincent Peale tells the story of a man who was so beside himself, he was contemplating suicide. He was older, and the business he had built was collapsing. He went to Peale saying, "Everything in my life is falling apart."

Peale questioned the man, in effect taking an inventory of his life. Peale learned, for instance, that the man still had a devoted wife and grown children who cared about him. His house and car had not been repossessed. His faith in God was still alive. After pointing out all this, Peale was able to help him get through his depression.

The point is, when failure comes, count your blessings. Then ask yourself, "What am I going to learn from this failure?" Immediately set some goals that will help you back onto the success track. And then get to work.

Edison said that genius was 99 percent perspiration and 1 percent inspiration. Who ever invented the word "easy?" So far, there isn't much I've encountered that is easy. I used to have an illusion that executives sat behind their desks with their feet up. That's bunk. It takes a tremendous amount of effort to achieve.

And does pursuing goals make a person happy?

If you're smart enough to attach yourself to an idea bigger than yourself. People who do this are enthusiastic. Look at how people volunteer for political campaigns and at hospitals. Why? Because there's something greater than themselves at stake. I feel strongly that the self*less* person, the person who spends his or her life giving to others, is the one who will have the best life.

Companies that give to their employees and to their customers, companies that love their customers and serve them with wholehearted dedication, are going to excel because of that caring. This holds true for individuals, too. Loving your "neighbor," whoever that neighbor is, is a worthy life goal. This is, by the way, what Jesus taught — loving and giving to others.

If I say, "Today my objective is serving my customers with the best tea that we can possibly make, and serving our stores with the best programs we can produce," I can be much more effective than if I walk in every day and say, "What am I going to do for myself? How much money am I going to make off those people today?" If my concern is on how good the tea is, how people are reacting to it, and what they need, I am dedicating myself to service. Generally, that mindset leads to success.

Tied in with service is quality. Frank Perdue, the king of the poultry business, says the question is not "How good *is* it?" but "How good *can* it be?" At Celestial Seasonings we're constantly going back and improving our products. And I really feel that that's part of life's quest for excellence.

Some people say, if it ain't broke, why fix it? I think the question is, what level of excellence can you reach? Growth starts with the state of mind which says: In relationship to the universe I am just a child. I know very little. I will keep my mind, my soul, and my spirit growing.

But to really go anywhere, that growth cannot be just one track. A person who is totally religious, and has no intellectual life, can become a boring fanatic. A person who is totally materialistic, but has no spiritual life, can be boringly wrapped up in material things. The most ideal growth I can imagine is one in which a human being develops in mind, spirit, and body.

I think it's sad to hear people say that once you're past forty, it's all downhill in business. That doesn't make sense. Very few chairmen of corporations are in their thirties or even in their forties. Most are in their fifties and sixties.

I imagine I will peak at fifty-five or sixty. My energy may go down, but my mind, my intellectual capacity, will have grown dramatically. I'll be better at cutting through the clutter then. I won't do some of the dumb things I did when I was younger. My hope for the world is, "Hey, let's all grow." Maybe then we'll warm up by the time we're sixty.

What have you learned this year?

For one thing, I've gone from just being good at word processing to becoming very good at computer graphics and computer drawing systems. I've also learned how to do data-based management on my computer.

I've read a number of books this year — some on the subject of families, others in the area of psychology. People ask, "Mo, have you changed?" I say, "I sure hope I have." Or they say, "Well, the company's really changed you."

Well, thank goodness. If I were the same as I was ten years ago, I'd be a pretty sad case of a human being. I hope I've changed.

How does your religious faith figure into your scheme of ideas about how people reach their potentials?

I think my faith's the most motivating factor in my life. I try to live by Jesus' teachings. Yet, I am not big on dogma, tradition, or ritual. I suppose my faith is slightly unorthodox in some people's views. I go to church but don't attend one church regularly, and I do not view the Bible as the only truth. I love the *Urantia* book and find wisdom in reading everything from Pierre Teilhard DeChardin to Kahlil Gibran. But if you don't have faith in God, how can you get up in the morning? How do people face the day without faith in something greater than themselves? Life is meaningful.

Love, to me, is the cornerstone of religion. As you move closer to God, you naturally become more loving. Part of my reason for reading books on psychology is the realization that if you want to love people, you have to understand them.

Which brings up another factor I'd like to mention. If you want to achieve your best, have a family. (Mo has three children, Gabe, Sarah, and Megan.) I'm not saying this categorically, but I think in general, we function best within a family. In the quest for equal rights, we've experienced some temporary disruption of the family. But I think as we accept equality, we will see a whole new definition of a woman's role within the world and within the family. And men will become full-fledged family members, as well as members of the work force. In other words, the family will not disappear, but it may take a slightly different form. Both sexes will have more freedom to be themselves within the family.

If you have a stable home life and are getting the fundamentals of love and warmth and caring — if you are learning to give to your children, learning to give to your husband or wife — you are a person who has the most potential for growing yourself.

Living in a family teaches you behavior modification, too. You can't just act like your crude self forever in a family. At some point you have to improve, and families can force you to a higher level.

Finally, never take yourself too seriously. There's a lot to laugh at —

our mistakes, the nature of our humanity . . . So we screw up sometimes. So what? Life is hard, but learning to smile helps us reach our potentials, and hurt a little less.

(Note: Kraft, Inc. bought Celestial Seasonings for over $35 million. Siegel resigned from Celestial Seasonings, announcing that he intended to devote his time to nonprofit work. Mo and Peggy Siegel were divorced, and Mo Siegel married Jennifer Cook on September 5, 1987.)

Unconventional Wisdom

After completing these conversations, I kept lingering over them, thinking about these people and all they had told me. I had deliberately sought out individuals who practice self-love and love for others. I had looked for those with the courage to voice their experiences. Beyond those two qualities, I did not expect other similarities, but I found them anyway, and it is likely that in your reading, you sensed them, too.

The seven attitudes that these diverse men and women share are not all-inclusive, and they are not like a grocery shopping list. You need not "buy" everything on it. But ponder these and pick up what you need or would like to cultivate in your own life.

The Common Attitudes

They search for meaning in their lives and find it.

They focus on the present.

They also have future goals and aspirations.

In trying to live each day wisely and in planning for the future, they choose priorities carefully.

They acknowledge and accept their limitations.

They face pain. They struggle with problems, but do not give up.

They experience great joy — in being alive and in being themselves.

Selected Reading

All of these books were consulted as I wrote this book. You will find quotes from many of them in these pages. In a myriad of ways, each adds some illumination to the subject of wisdom.

Adler, Mortimer J. *Ten Philosophical Mistakes (Basic Errors in Modern Thought — How They Came About, Their Consequences, and How to Avoid Them)*. New York: MacMillan Publishing Company, 1985.

Bartlett, John. *Familiar Quotations*. Boston: Little, Brown and Company, 1982.

Cousins, Norman. *Human Options*. New York: W.W. Norton and Company, 1981.

Dillard, Annie. *Pilgrim at Tinker Creek*. Toronto, Canada: Bantam Books, Inc., 1975.

Gibran, Kahlil. *The Prophet*. New York: Alfred A. Knopf, 1975. (Original copyright 1923 by Kahlil Gibran.)

Hammarskjold, Dag. *Markings*. New York: Alfred A. Knopf, 1967.

Harris, Sydney J. *Winners & Losers*. Niles, IL: Argus Communications, 1973.

Kennedy, Eugene. *Free to Be Human*. New York: Cornerstone Library, 1979.

Jourard, Sidney M. *The Transparent Self*. New York: D. Van Nostrand Company, 1971.

Kopp, Sheldon. *Even a Stone Can Be a Teacher (Learning and Growing from the Experiences of Everyday Life)*. Los Angeles: Jeremy P. Tarcher, Inc., 1985.

Kopp, Sheldon. *If You Meet the Buddha on the Road, Kill Him! (The Pilgrimage of Psychotherapy Patients)*. New York: Bantam Books, 1973.

Kushner, Harold S. *When Bad Things Happen to Good People*. New York: Avon Books, 1983.

Lamm, Dottie. *Second Banana*. Boulder, CO: Johnson Books, 1983.

Lindbergh, Anne Morrow. *War Within and Without (Diaries and Letters 1939-1944)*. New York: Harcourt Brace Jovanovich, 1980.

May, Rollo. *The Courage to Create*. New York: Bantam Books, 1975.

Merton, Thomas. *No Man Is An Island*. New York: Harcourt Brace Jovanovich, 1955.

Peck, M. Scott, M.D. *People of the Lie (The Hope for Healing Human Evil)*. New York: Simon and Schuster, 1983.

Peck, M. Scott, M.D. *The Road Less Traveled (A New Psychology of Love, Traditional Values and Spiritual Growth)*. New York: Simon and Schuster, 1978.

Prather, Hugh. *I Touch the Earth, The Earth Touches Me*. Garden City, NY: Doubleday & Company, Inc., 1972.

Reid, Clyde. *Celebrate the Temporary*. New York: Harper & Row, 1972.

Rilke, Rainer Maria. *Rilke on Love and Other Difficulties (Translations and Considerations of Rainer Maria Rilke by John J.L. Mood)*. New York: W. W. Norton & Company, 1975.

Rubin, Theodore Isaac, M.D. *Reconciliations — Inner Peace in an Age of Anxiety*. New York: The Viking Press, 1980.

Tillich, Paul. *The Courage to Be*. New Haven, CN: Yale University Press, 1952.

Tournier, Paul. *The Gift of Feeling*. Atlanta, GA: John Knox Press, 1981.

Tyler, Robert. *Better Than Rubies — 30 Centuries of Collected Wisdom*. Denver, CO: Logos, Ltd., 1984.

Ullmann, Liv. *Choices*. New York: Alfred A. Knopf, 1984.

Wilhelm, Richard (Translation), rendered into English by Cary F. Baynes. *The I Ching (Book of Changes)*. Princeton, NJ: Princeton University Press, 1950.

Holy Bible (Revised Standard Version).

About the Author

Pat Quigley won the 1982 and 1983 awards for the Best Personality Profiles in *Colorado Homes and Lifestyles* magazine. She is the author of *Creative Writing: A Handbook for Teaching Classes Wherever Adults Gather* and *Creative Writing II: A Handbook of Techniques for Effective Writing*. More than two hundred of her articles, essays, poems, and book reviews have appeared in regional, national, and international publications.

She is married to Jack Quigley and has two sons, Matt and Tim.